IS-30.B: Mitigation eGrants System for the Subgrant Applicant

By

Fema

1/10/2018

Course Overview

This course is part of the comprehensive training program for the FEMA eGrants system. This course is the first in the series of Independent Study (IS) courses for eGrants and will address the functions in the eGrants External System used by Subapplicants. The purpose of this course is to provide you with the knowledge to:

- Complete a subapplication in eGrants
- Review a subapplication in eGrants
- Submit a subapplication to an Applicant using eGrants
- Check the status of a subapplication in eGrants
- Revise a subapplication in eGrants

Terms Used in this Course

The Office of Management and Budget streamlined the Federal Government's Administrative Requirements, Cost Principles, and Audit Requirements for Federal Awards into a consolidated set of regulations. These regulations are located in Title 2 of the Code of Federal Regulations, Part 200, and are referred to as the "Super Circular." The Super Circular also introduced new terminology, including "Recipient" instead of "Grantee" and "Subrecipient" instead of "Subgrantee."

Because terminology has changed, many of the terms used in the eGrants Internal and External Systems screens are not consistent with the current terms used in the Super Circular. This course will reference eGrants screen labels as they appear, but will use Super Circular terminology throughout the rest of the course. Below is a table to assist you in understanding the terminology you will encounter in this course.

Super Circular	eGrants Screens	Definition
Federal Award	Grant	The federal financial assistance received directly from FEMA
Subaward	Subgrant	The federal financial assistance received indirectly from a pass-through entity (Applicant to a Subapplicant)
Applicant	Applicant or Grant Applicant	A state agency, territorial government, or federally-recognized tribal government submitting an application to FEMA

		for assistance under FEMA's hazard mitigation grant programs
Subapplicant	Subgrant Applicant	A state agency, local government, territorial government, federally-recognized tribal government, or qualified private non-profit organization submitting a subapplication to an Applicant for assistance under FEMA's hazard mitigation grant programs
Application	Grant Application	Application for federal financial assistance directly from FEMA
Subapplication	Subgrant Application	Application for federal financial assistance indirectly through a pass-through entity (Subapplicant to Applicant, Applicant to FEMA)
Recipient	Grantee	An Applicant whose application has been approved and a federal award obligated
Subrecipient	Subgrantee	A Subapplicant whose subapplication has been approved and a subaward obligated

Lesson Overview

This lesson provides an overview of the course and an introduction to various course features and functionality.

At the end of the lesson, you should be able to describe the:

- Course structure
- Course navigation
- Knowledge Check functionality
- Slideshow functionality
- Screen features and navigation tools

Course Structure

Take a moment to review the lesson plan for this course. The lesson plan is labeled **Lesson List** and is located on the right side of your screen.

This course contains nine lessons. The lessons may be accessed sequentially or independently. The time to complete each lesson varies. A page tracker is displayed at the bottom middle of the screen to help you gauge your movement through the lesson. The estimated time required to complete each lesson will be stated on the lesson's first screen.

After completing the course, take the Final Exam to:

- Gauge your knowledge of the topic
- Receive credit for taking the course

Lesson 1 Summary

You have completed the first lesson. In this lesson, you learned about:

- The goals and structure of the course
- How to navigate within the course using screen features and your keyboard
- How to access slideshows
- How to interact with Knowledge Checks

Remember, you must complete all lessons and pass the Final Exam to receive credit for the course.

Now that we have introduced the course goals and discussed the various navigation elements and features of the course, let's get started. To begin the course, select the **Next** button or choose a lesson from the **Topic** drop-down list.

Lesson 2 Overview

When we're done with this lesson, you'll be able to:

- Identify the purpose of eGrants and the FEMA mitigation grant programs it supports
- Identify the categories of eGrants users
- Identify the steps and possible outcomes of the subapplication process within eGrants

The Purpose of eGrants

State and territorial governments, federally-recognized tribal governments, and local governments use an "external" version of eGrants to:

- Apply electronically for assistance through the Flood Mitigation Assistance (FMA) and Pre-Disaster Mitigation (PDM) grant programs
- Electronically manage their FMA and PDM applications and subapplications
- Electronically manage federal awards and subawards for the FMA and PDM grant programs, as well as the legacy Repetitive Flood Claims (RFC) and Severe Repetitive Loss (SRL) grant programs.

FEMA uses an "internal" version of eGrants to review submitted applications and subapplications.

Select an official from each government to learn more about how they use the eGrants system.

<u>Listen to the Local Official</u> <u>Listen to the State Official</u> <u>Listen to the FEMA Official</u>

Local Government Official **State Government Official** **FEMA Official**

<u>Select this link to access a transcript of all audio files on this screen.</u>

eGrants Users Summary

Local Government Official:
Local governments like ours, and some federally-recognized tribal governments, use eGrants to create and submit pre-applications to Applicants in state, territorial, and federally-recognized tribal governments, if they require them. Pre-applications only apply to project subapplications and, if required, must be approved prior to being granted permission to create and submit a subapplication. After our pre-application is approved, we can use eGrants to create and submit a subapplication to the Applicant.

State Government Official:
As Applicants, we use eGrants to manage Subapplicant user access, and to review and process subapplications. If we approve a subapplication, we attach it to our application and submit it to FEMA. If we don't approve a subapplication, we may stockpile it for future consideration or we may ask the Subapplicant to revise and resubmit it. We can also create our own subapplications and include them in our application. FEMA may request revisions to our application or to a subapplication. For revisions to a subapplication, we can either make the changes ourselves or we can release the subapplication back to the Subapplicant and ask them to make the revisions. For revisions to an application, we'll just make them ourselves and

resubmit the application back to FEMA for review. If FEMA obligates our federal award, we can view the award package in eGrants. Afterwards, we use eGrants to submit our Quarterly Performance Reports to FEMA.

FEMA Official:
We use eGrants to manage Applicant user access and to review subapplications and applications for completeness, award eligibility, cost-effectiveness, the cost of the proposed project, and to document the status of Applicant mitigation plans. If we approve an application, we process it and the associated subapplications for federal award. We may make amendments to the award package later. If we don't approve a subapplication, we may ask the Applicant to make revisions and to resubmit the subapplication. After we obligate a federal award, we monitor its status by reviewing the quarterly performance and financial reports that the Applicant submits to us.

Types of Grant Programs

As a Subapplicant, you'll be able to use eGrants to create, submit, and manage subapplications for the two Hazard Mitigation Assistance (HMA) grant programs that eGrants supports:

Flood Mitigation Assistance (FMA)—The FMA grant program was created to reduce or eliminate claims under the National Flood Insurance Program (NFIP). FMA federal awards provide funding to assist communities in implementing measures to reduce or eliminate long-term risks of flood damage.
Learn more about the FMA grant program at URL https://www.fema.gov/flood-mitigation-assistance-grant-program

Pre-Disaster Mitigation (PDM)—Funding for the PDM grant program is provided to assist local, state, territorial, and federally-recognized tribal governments in implementing cost-effective hazard mitigation activities.

Learn more about the PDM grant program at URL https://www.fema.gov/pre-disaster-mitigation-grant-program

Pre-applications

In some cases, the first step in the subapplication process is the completion of a pre-application. However, pre-applications are not required by all Applicants. Applicants determine when—or if—this requirement is appropriate. If pre-applications are required, this requirement applies to all Subapplicants within the Applicant's state, territorial, or tribal area.

When pre-applications are required, they are only required for project subapplications. If a pre-application is required, it will appear as a menu option at the beginning of the eGrants process. If it's not required, it will not appear.

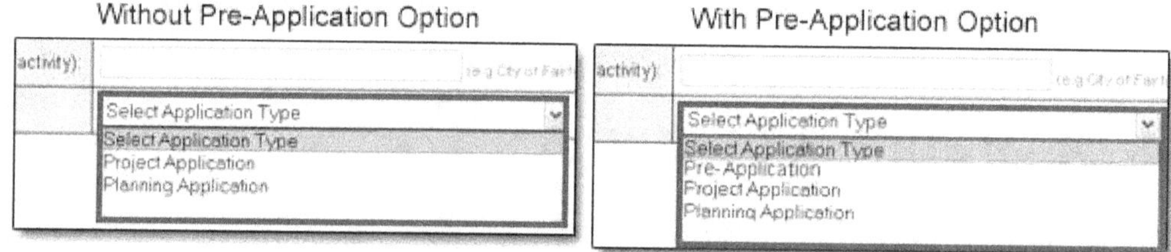

Select this link for the full text of the image.

How Subapplications Are Processed

The application process in eGrants follows a specific work flow:

- Initially, a Subapplicant creates a subapplication and submits it to the appropriate Applicant for review.
- Next, an Applicant official reviews the subapplication. He or she may request revisions.
- If revisions are requested, the Subapplicant may revise the subapplication and resubmit it.
- Once the subapplication is reviewed and complete, the Applicant may include it in a larger application that is submitted to FEMA.
- Subapplications not selected to be included in an application may be "stockpiled," or retained for future consideration.

Select this link to view a diagram of the subapplication process in another window.

Application Process Flow Diagram

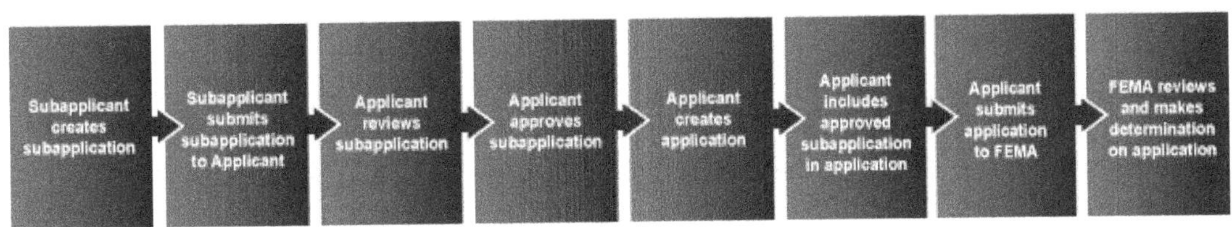

In this diagram, the following steps in the application process are shown:

- Subapplicant creates subapplication
- Subapplicant submits subapplication to Applicant
- Applicant reviews subapplication
- Applicant approves subapplication
- Applicant includes approved subapplication in application
- Applicant submits the application to FEMA
- FEMA reviews and makes determination on application

Note When an Applicant submits an application, FEMA reviews the application and its subapplications and, if necessary, asks the Applicant to make revisions to subapplications. The Applicant may make the requested revisions or may ask the Subapplicant to revise the subapplication.

Lesson 2 Summary

Let's review what you learned in Lesson 2:

- eGrants allows users to create, submit, review, and process subapplications and applications.
- FMA and PDM subapplications and applications can be processed using eGrants.
- SRL and RFC legacy federal awards and subawards can be managed using eGrants.
- Applicant users include state, territorial, and federally-recognized tribal government officials.
- Subapplicants include local government and federally-recognized tribal government officials.
- The eGrants workflow involves the creation and submission of a subapplication to the Applicant. The Applicant may then include that subapplication in the larger application that it submits to FEMA.

Lesson 3 Overview

Upon completion of this lesson, you will be able to:

- Identify the steps in the eGrants registration process

eGrants User Scenario

This course will cover the creation of a subapplication in FEMA's eGrants system. As part of this course, you will participate in a scenario in which you are a first-time user of eGrants.

You will be assisting your boss, Sally Watkins, the City Manager for River City in the State of Columbia, by using eGrants to create a Flood Mitigation Assistance (FMA) subapplication.

River City wants to acquire three properties that are located in the floodplain of the South Branch of the Washburn River. Several properties have been affected by repeated flooding. River City wishes to apply for a subaward to acquire and demolish the residential structures and convert the area to a community park. As the city has plans for more acquisitions when additional funds become available, the project is called "River City Floodplain Acquisition—Phase 1."

Select this link to see the map of River City.

Select this link for the full text of the map of River City.

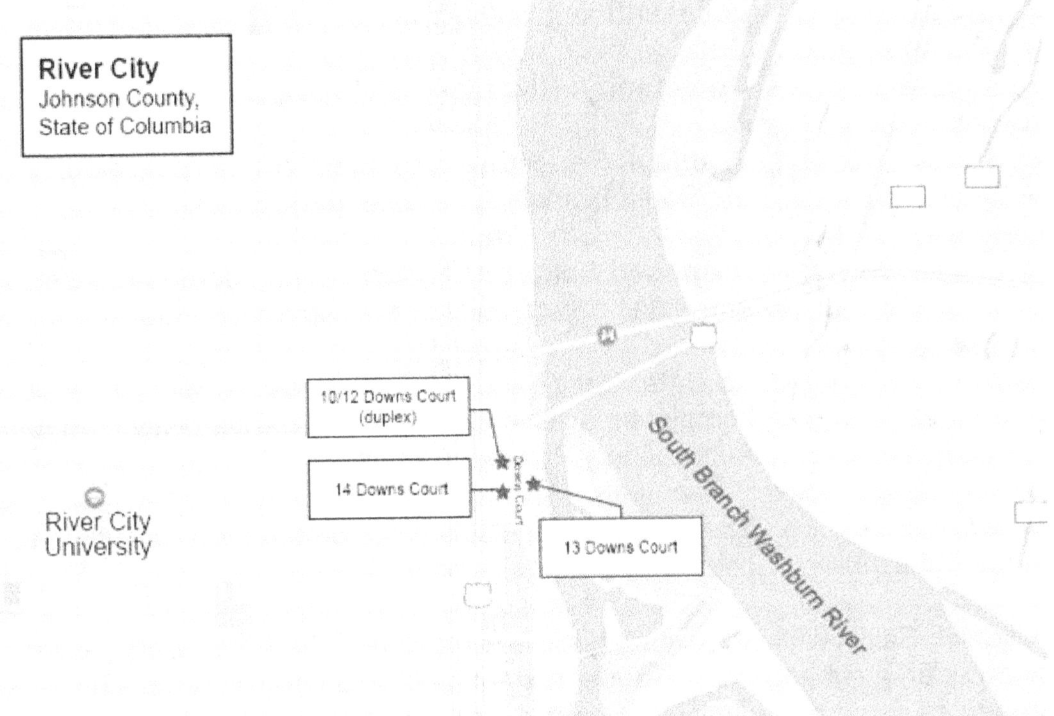

River City Map Description

Map of River City, State of Columbia. The map title: River City, Johnson County, State of Columbia appears in a box in the upper left quadrant. The South Branch of the Washburn River runs from north to south through the middle of the image. River City University is indicated by a mortar board icon in the lower left quadrant. In the middle of the map, along the left bank of the Washburn River, are three red stars with labels indicating the properties slated for acquisition and demolition: 10/12 Downs Court (duplex), 14 Downs Court, and 13 Downs Court. City streets are marked as white lines and travel north to south, and east to west on the West bank of the Washburn River. Downs Court is labeled and runs north/south on the west bank of the river. Yellow lines indicating two highways cross horizontally and vertically below the property labels. Parkland is indicated in green.

Acquisition Scenario

Local Official: Sally Watkins

Community: River City, State of Columbia

Problem: Repetitive flooding of three properties along the South Branch of the Washburn River

Proposed Solution: To acquire and demolish the properties and replace them with a community park

To Date: Sally has asked you to assist her with completing a subapplication for the River City Floodplain Acquisition—Phase 1 project.

Listen to Sally
Audio transcript

Your Next Step: You will become familiar with how to navigate within eGrants.

Hello. I'm Sally Watkins, River City's City Manager. This month we'll be working together on a subapplication requesting funds to acquire and demolish properties in our community that have experienced repeat flooding. When the subapplication is complete, I'll submit it to the State of Columbia. Hopefully, Columbia will include it in its application to FEMA. Right now, I'm just starting the process, so I'll need you to register to use eGrants before we can begin the subapplication.

eGrants Registration Process

The registration process is required before attempting to access eGrants for the first time.

This process involves four steps:

- You need to contact the appropriate Applicant official to receive an Access Identification (ID) code. This step prevents unauthorized individuals from clogging the system with bogus User ID requests.
- Use the FEIMS registration screens to create an account.
- Once your FEIMS account has been created, you need to request privileges to access eGrants. The Applicant official will approve or reject this request. If your request is rejected, you will not be permitted to access eGrants.
- If the request is approved, you will receive an e-mail notification which authorizes you to create, submit, and/or manage subapplications in eGrants.

Setting Up a FEIMS Account

Since we already have an Access ID number from our Applicant, the Columbia Department of Emergency Management, you now need to set up your FEIMS account.

- Open your browser.
- Type in the _FEIMS_ URL: https://portal.fema.gov/famsVuWeb/home. **Bookmark this site to avoid having to re-type the URL.**
- Since this is the first time you are logging into eGrants and because you don't have a Personal Identification Verification (PIV) card, select the **New Non-PIV User?** button.

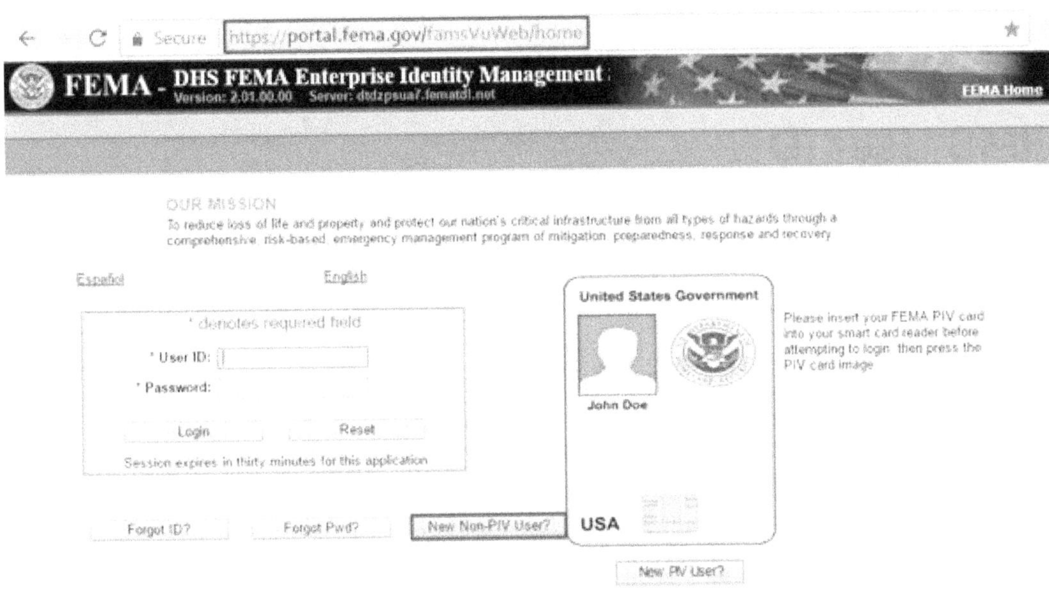

Select this link for the full text of the image.

FEIMS Security Question

To enter the FEIMS system, you must complete the security check question by entering into the text box the letters shown in the graphic and selecting the Submit button.

This will help protect your information from automated attacks.

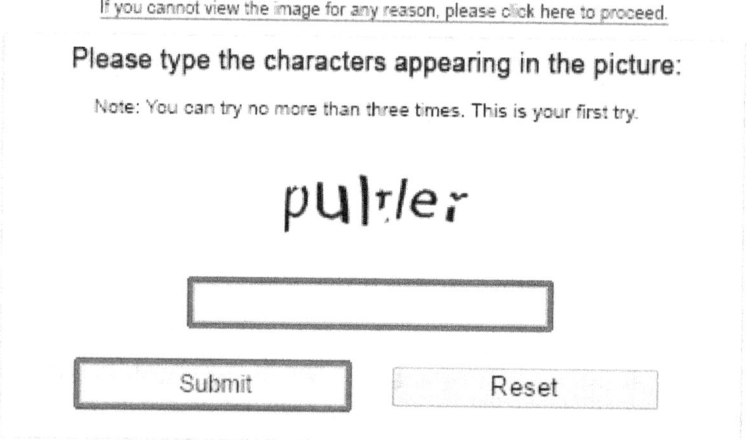

Select this link for the full text of the image.

FEIMS User ID

During the registration process, you must create a unique FEIMS User ID. This User ID should be something you can remember and must also meet the following criteria:

- All ID letters should be lowercase
- The ID must have a minimum of seven characters
- The ID cannot exceed a maximum of 10 characters
- The ID must not contain any special characters (e.g., %, $, or ?)

Subapplicants need to check with their Applicant official to learn of any required naming conventions for their area. Our Applicant doesn't have any special requirements, so you can use **rivercity2** as your User ID.

FEIMS Password

During the registration process, you must create a unique FEIMS password in addition to your User ID. This password should as be something you can remember and must meet the following criteria:

- The password must contain a minimum of eight characters
- The password may not contain special characters (e.g., #, @, or ?)

For security reasons, it is recommended that you change your password every 30 to 90 days.

If you believe your FEIMS password has been compromised, immediately notify your Applicant.

Organization Search

To complete the FEIMS registration form you will need to complete the Contact(s) section. This is where you identify the name of your organization, River City.

It is important to ensure that everyone within the same organization inputs the name consistently. To guarantee that this happens, rather than typing in the organization name, you should search the system to find the name as it already appears.

To locate the name of your organization in FEIMS:

- Select the Search link in the Contact(s) section.
- Type the first few letters of your organization's name in the Organization text field.
- Select the Search button.

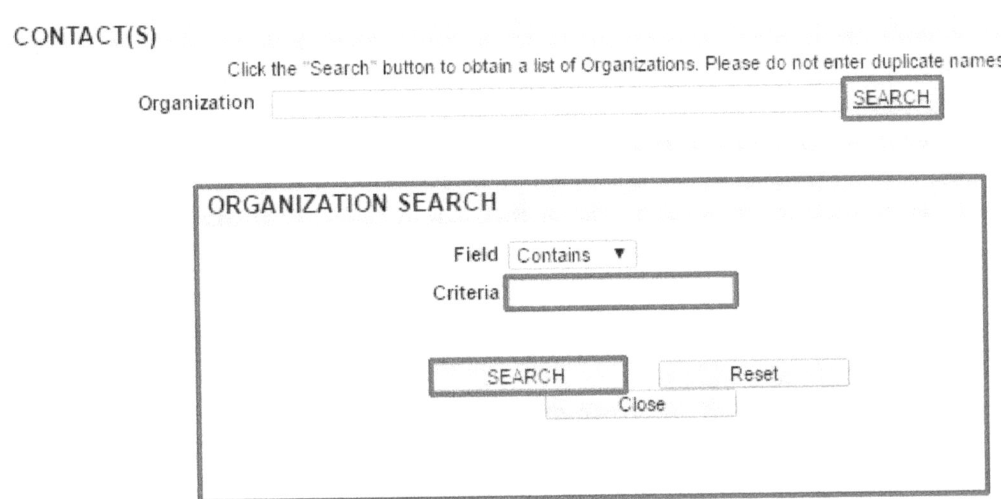

Select this link for the full text of the image.

Requesting Privileges

Once you have completed all of the fields in the Registration Form and created
a User ID and a password, your FEIMS account will be created.

You will then need to request privileges for access to eGrants by selecting
the "Click here to request new privileges" link.

Select this link for the full text of the image.

Note If you do not request privileges at the time your FEIMS account is
created, you can log in at another time using the same User ID and
password you created and request privileges then.

Requesting Access to eGrants

When the Available Applications screen displays:

- Select the Request Access button to the right of the Mitigations eGrants
  Application icon.
- Type your Access ID in the text entry field and select Submit.

You will need to wait for our Applicant, the Columbia Department of Emergency
Management, to approve your request for eGrants access.

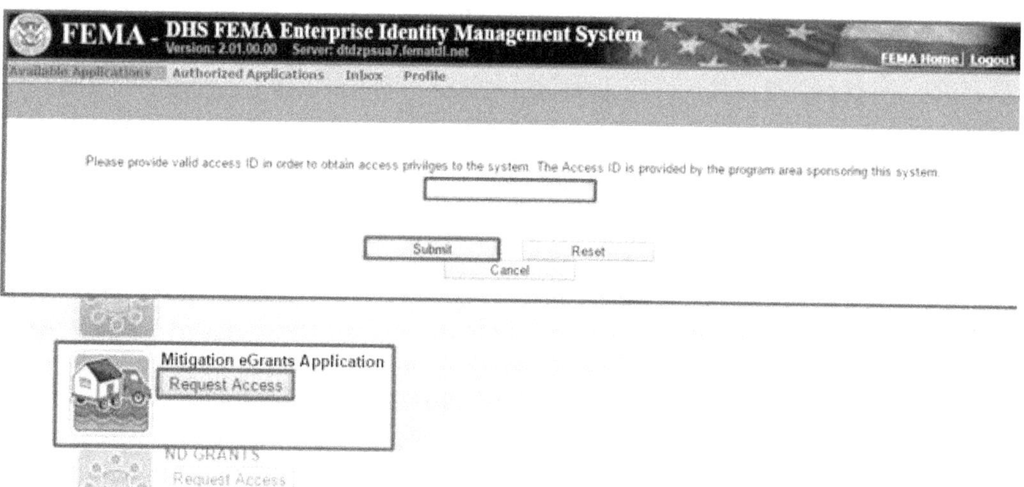

Select this link for the full text of the image.

Access Levels

There are three access levels that a Registered User may be given:

- **View/Print:** This level means that you have the ability to view and print subapplications and/or applications in eGrants.
- **Create/Edit:** This level means that you have the ability to do the above tasks and also to create, update, and change subapplications and/or applications in eGrants.
- **Sign/Submit:** This level means that you have the ability to do all of the above tasks and also to sign and submit applications to FEMA.

Approval E-mail

The final step in the eGrants registration process is receiving an e-mail from the Applicant official. In our case, the e-mail will come from someone at the Columbia Department of Emergency Management. The e-mail will be an official record of approval of your access to the eGrants system and may include information about the specific role assigned to you in the system.

Select this link to view a sample eGrants access approval e-mail.

To:	michael.johnson@rivercity.gov
Date:	03-17-2017
Subject:	Registration Approved
From:	ramirezr@cl.gov
Body:	Your request for access to the FEMA Mitigation eGrants System has been approved.

Select this link for the full text of the image.

Note You will not receive an e-mail immediately. If you have not received an e-mail, it is likely that your registration request has not yet been reviewed.

Log into eGrants and Request Access

Now that you're approved, you can log into and access the eGrants system.

If you bookmarked the <u>FEIMS login page</u> at URL https://portal.fema.gov/famsVuWeb/home, you can select the bookmark to open it in your browser.

Scroll down to see slideshow captions.

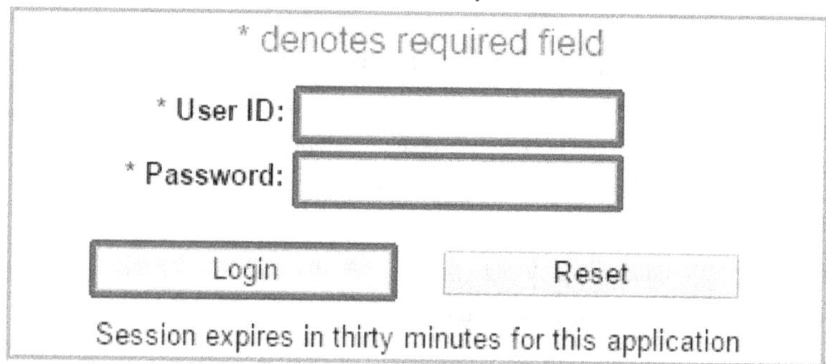

The FEIMS login screen will ask you to enter your **User ID** and **Password**. Then, select the **Login** button.

Select the **Request Access** button on the right of the Mitigation eGrants Application icon.

To complete the request, you need to type the Access ID provided by provided by our FEMA Regional Office in the appropriate field and select the **Submit** button. You need to remember that creating a FEIMS account does not automatically generate access to eGrants.

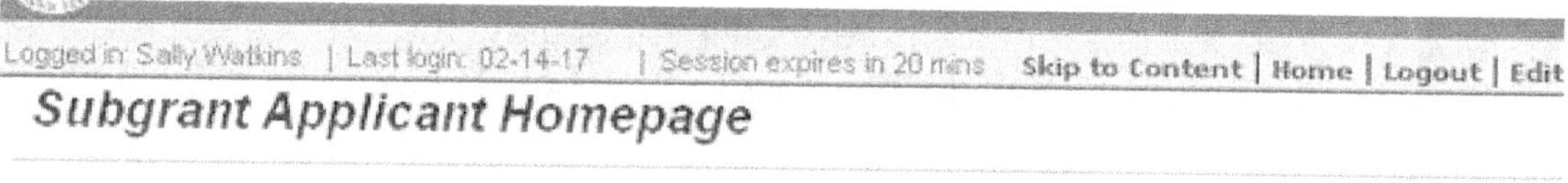

When you successfully log into eGrants, the Subgrant Applicant Homepage appears.

Editing Your Profile

If any of your personal information, such as your phone number or e-mail address, changes after you've registered, you can update it by selecting the Edit Profile link in the upper right corner of the Subgrant Applicant Homepage.

<u>Select this link for the full text of the image.</u>

Logging Out

When you are finished working in eGrants, you will need to exit the system by logging out. There is a right way and wrong way to log out.

Right way
The right way to log out is to either select the **Logout** link that appears in the upper right-hand corner of all eGrants screens or the **Logout** button at the bottom left of some eGrants screens.

Wrong way
The wrong way to log out is to select the X button in the upper right corner of your browser window. While this will close the eGrants window, it will not necessarily end the eGrants session, and you will lose any data you entered on the current screen.

Lesson 3 Summary

In Lesson 3 you learned:

- The first step in setting up a FEIMS account is to request an Access ID from the Applicant.
- Requests for access to eGrants must be approved by the Applicant.
- You can update your personal information after registration by selecting the Edit Profile link on the eGrants Subgrant Applicant Homepage.
- Different access levels in eGrants provide the user with different privileges.
- To log out of eGrants, always select either the Logout link in the upper right hand corner of the screen or the Logout button, if it is available on the screen.

Lesson 4 Overview

When you are done with this lesson, you will be able to:

- Identify the eGrants system screen features and their uses

Acquisition Scenario

Name: Sally Watkins

Community: River City, State of Columbia

Problem: Repetitive flooding of three properties along the South Branch of the Washburn River

Proposed Solution: To acquire and demolish the properties and replace them with a community park

To Date: Sally has asked you to assist her with completing a subapplication for the River City Floodplain Acquisition—Phase 1 project.

The Next Step: Sally will show you how to create a FEMA Enterprise Identity Management System (FEIMS) User ID and password and request access to the eGrants system.

Listen to Sally
Audio transcript

Hello. I'm Sally Watkins, and this month you'll be working with me on a subapplication. When it's complete, I'll submit it to the State of Columbia. The State will, hopefully, include it in its application to FEMA. Right now, you've just logged in to eGrants for the first time, so you'll need to learn how to use the system before beginning the subapplication.

Navigation Buttons

Navigating within eGrants is like navigating within other Web-based applications by using navigation features such as links, buttons, and scrollbars.

Buttons

Users may select a button to perform a specific function. There are several buttons that appear throughout the eGrants system. **Select a button** to view a description of its function.

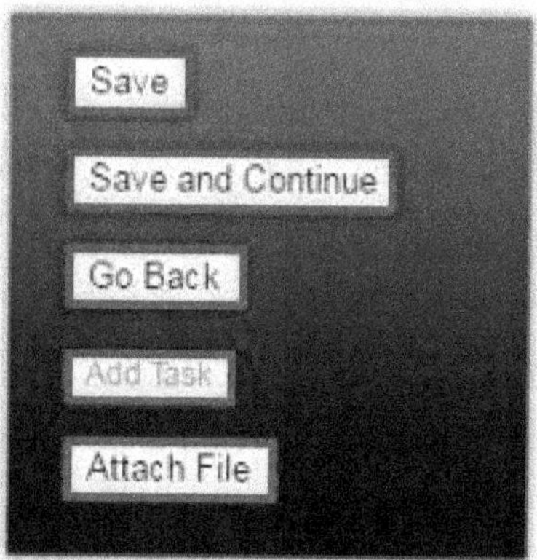

Select this link to view a summary of the information presented.

Summary of Navigation Buttons

Save: Stores data from the current screen into the eGrants system.

Save and Continue: Stores data from the current screen into the eGrants system and advances to the next screen.

Go Back: Used to return to the previous screen without losing data entered.

Add Task (dimmed): Sometimes a button will appear gray and dim. A dimmed button is not active and indicates that you must complete a task before it is reactivated.

Attach File: Initiates the option to select a file to be attached to a subapplication.

Entering Information

Entering information within eGrants is similar to entering information within other web-based applications. There are two primary ways to enter data in eGrants:

Drop-down menus
These fields offer users the opportunity to select an item from a limited list. First, **select the arrow** at the right of the field to see the list and then select the appropriate item from the list.

Text fields
These fields provide the opportunity to input data by typing. Simply place the cursor at the beginning of the field and use the keyboard to **type the appropriate information.** If the data must be entered in a specific format, an example of that format will be shown next to the text field.

Note	Required fields are marked by an asterisk (*). You don't have to complete the required fields to move on to another section; however, you cannot successfully submit a subapplication if you haven't completed all of the required fields in every section.

Saving Information

To ensure that information you have entered into eGrants is successfully captured, it is essential to save your data. At the bottom of each screen are two buttons that can be used to save data. Failure to use the **Save** buttons will result in the loss of all data entered since the last time the subapplication was saved.

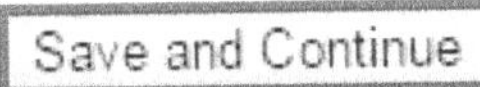

Save and Continue
This feature saves the data entered in the current section of the subapplication and automatically advances the user to the next section of the subapplication.

Save
This feature saves the data entered in the current section of the subapplication but does not automatically advance the user to the next section of the subapplication.

Avoid Losing Information

The information that you have entered into eGrants could be lost for two reasons:

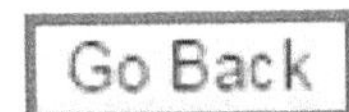

Browser buttons
Using the Back and Next buttons on your browser toolbar will result in data loss. You should only use the Save, Save and Continue, and Go Back buttons within eGrants. Using these buttons will ensure that information entered is saved and stored in eGrants.

Session expiration
Each eGrants session expires after 20 minutes of inactivity. The time remaining until the session expires is displayed at the top left corner of the eGrants screen. If no activity has occurred within a 20-minute timeframe, you will be disconnected from the system and you must log in again to resume processing. All unsaved data will be lost when the session expires.

Scrolling

Another navigation feature in eGrants is the scrollbar located along the right edge of any screen that requires scrolling to see the entire page. The scrollbar enables you to move up and down in screens that are longer than your Internet browser's window.

To use the scrollbar, just select the arrow at either the top or bottom of the scrollbar. Another option is to select the scrollbar itself and drag it in the direction you want the screen to move.

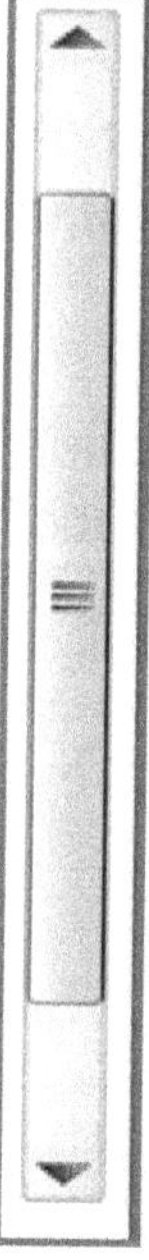

Hyperlinks

eGrants also utilizes hyperlinks to provide more information. They are displayed in blue underlined text or designated as links for those using assistive technology.

- **Hyperlinks** open a new window that displays additional information without taking you away from your current screen in eGrants.
- **Help links** are a special kind of hyperlink that displays a pop-up window with details about the information you need to enter into a text field. Help links appear to the right of the field as the word "Help" in blue, underlined text.

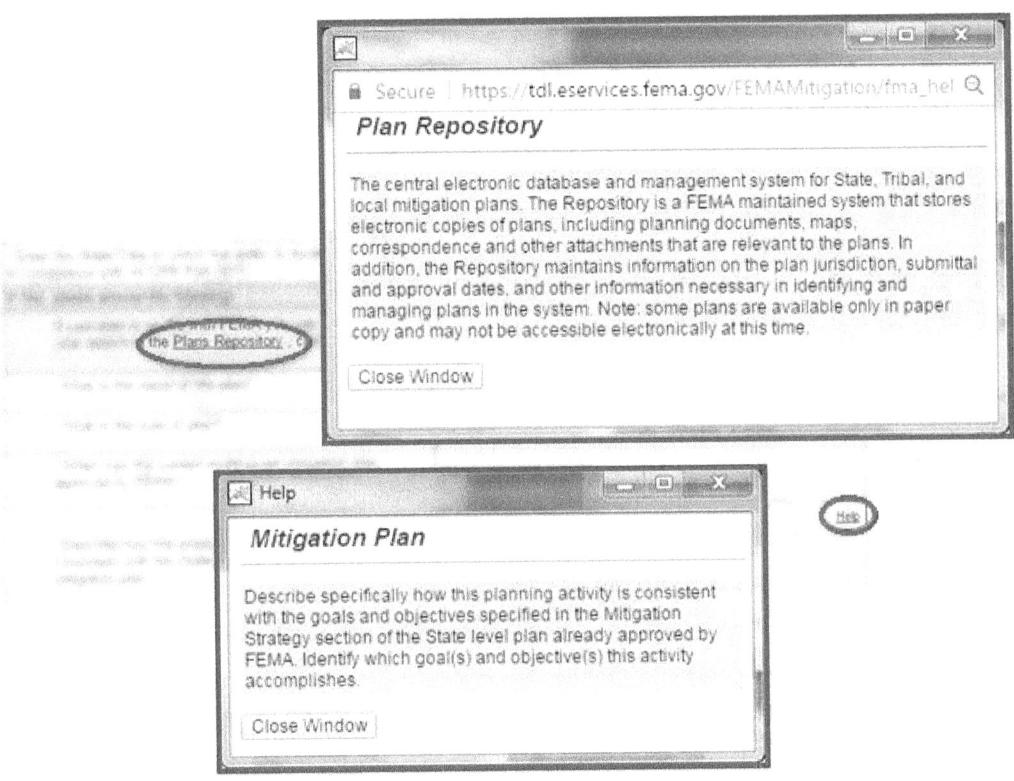

<u>Select this link for the full text of the image.</u>

Main Menu

There are three types of menus within eGrants:

- Main menu
- Task menus
- Sidebar menu

The main menu appears at the bottom of the eGrants screen.

FEMA Home

This feature moves the eGrants user to the FEMA Homepage.

eGrants Home

This feature moves the eGrants user to the Subgrant Applicant Homepage.

Contact Us

This feature opens a new window offering FEMA phone numbers and an online information request form.

Glossary

This feature opens a new window offering an extensive, alphabetized list of eGrants terms and definitions.

Help

This feature opens a new window offering information for first-time eGrants users, as well as definitions of technical concepts related to eGrants use.

Task Menus

Task menus, such as those found on the Subgrant Applicant Homepage, allow you to navigate to a particular task to perform.

In the example below, you have four task options from which to choose.

Print Blank Applications
Create New Application
Update/Complete Un-submitted Application(s)
Revise/Amend Submitted Application(s)

Sidebar Menu

The sidebar menu appears on the left side of subapplication screens.

Selecting the hyperlinked name of a section allows you to jump right to that section of the subapplication without having to move through all the sections sequentially.

Select this link for a full description of the sidebar image.

Lesson 4 Summary

You have completed the Navigation within eGrants lesson. Let's review what you learned:

- You primarily enter data in eGrants using drop-down menus and text entry fields.
- Use the scrollbar to view all the information on one page
- Select the hyperlinks and Help links for additional information.
- Use the main menu, task menus, and sidebar menu to accomplish other navigation and data entry tasks.
- Required fields are marked with an asterisk (*).
- To avoid losing information, you should always use the Save or Save and Continue buttons.
- After 20 minutes of inactivity, eGrants will close the session and any unsaved data will be lost.

Lesson 5 Overview

When you are done with this lesson, you will be able to:
- Identify the types of subapplications
- Identify the advantages and disadvantages of copying existing subapplications in eGrants

Acquisition Scenario

Name: Sally Watkins

Community: River City, State of Columbia

Problem: Repetitive flooding of three properties along the South Branch of the Washburn River

Proposed Solution: To acquire and demolish the properties and replace them with a community park

To Date: You have registered for and accessed FEMA's eGrants system. You have familiarized yourself with the navigation features.

Listen to Sally
Audio transcript

Your Next Step: You will create a subapplication.

Hello. I'm Sally Watkins and I am the River City City Manager. Today, we'll be creating a subapplication asking for funds to acquire and demolish properties in the floodplain of the Washburn River. So far, you've registered and logged into the eGrants system. Now, I'm going to show you how to create the subapplication.

Subapplication Types

It is important to know which type of subapplication is being proposed because the sections required for each type varies.

Select this link for a chart of the required subapplication sections.

There are four types of subapplications in the eGrants system:

Project: Project subapplications are completed for any mitigation measure or activity proposed to reduce the risk of future damage, hardship, loss, or suffering. Typically, projects are "brick and mortar" construction or a type of physical measures. Examples of activities that are eligible project types are acquisition, elevation, or relocation of flood-prone properties or retrofitting buildings to withstand wind or seismic events. There are also other mitigation activities that may be considered. For a complete list, please refer to the latest Hazard Mitigation Assistance (HMA) Guidance and Addendum at URL https://www.fema.gov/hazard-mitigation-assistance-program-guidance. A FEMA-approved hazard mitigation plan is required to receive a project subaward.

Planning: Planning subapplications are completed for local, state, territorial, federally recognized tribal, or multi-jurisdictional mitigation planning activities that will result in the creation of a new or updated mitigation plan. Planning subapplications are for completing mitigation plans that demonstrate the Subapplicant's commitment to reducing risks from natural hazards and serve as a guide for decision makers as they commit resources. A FEMA-approved hazard mitigation plan is not required to be able to receive a planning subaward.

Required Sections for Subapplications

	Project	Planning	Management Costs	Technical Assistance
Subapplicant	X	X	X	X
Contact	X	X	X	X
Community	X	X	X	X
Mitigation Plan	X	X		
Scope of Work	X	X	X	X
Properties	X			
Schedule	X	X	X	X
Cost Estimate	X	X	X	X
Cost Share	X		X	X
Cost Effectiveness	X			

Environmental/Historic Preservation	x			
Evaluation	x	x		
Assurances and Certification	x	x	x	x
Comments and Attachments	x	x	x	x

Subapplication Types (continued)

Management Costs: Management costs subapplications are completed by Applicants for activities that are directly related to the administration of programs or promotion of mitigation activities and may include outreach and training, environmental or historic preservation reviews, developing subapplications, performing Benefit-Cost Analyses, etc.

Technical Assistance: Technical assistance subapplications are completed by Applicants for activities that promote the Flood Mitigation Assistance (FMA) program to communities.

Note Management costs subapplications are available only for Applicants. Applicants must complete a separate management costs subapplication to apply for their management costs. However, Subapplicant management cost activities, if necessary, are to be included in the Subapplicant's project or planning subapplication.

Note Technical assistance subapplications are available only to Applicants acting as Subapplicants.

Creating a New Subapplication

One of the options listed in the task menu on the Subgrant Applicant Homepage is **Create New Application.** This option allows you to create a blank subapplication into which you will enter all the appropriate data.

For the acquisition scenario, starting with a blank subapplication is appropriate. Sally has all the necessary data for you to input. In the slideshow below, Sally demonstrates how to create a new subapplication.

Scroll down to see slideshow captions.

<table>
<tr><td>In some cases, the first step in the process of preparing a project subapplication is completing a pre-application. However, pre-applications are not required by all Applicants. Applicants determine if or when this requirement is appropriate. If pre-applications are required, the requirement applies to all eGrant users within the Applicant's state, territory, or tribal area.</td></tr>
</table>

Note

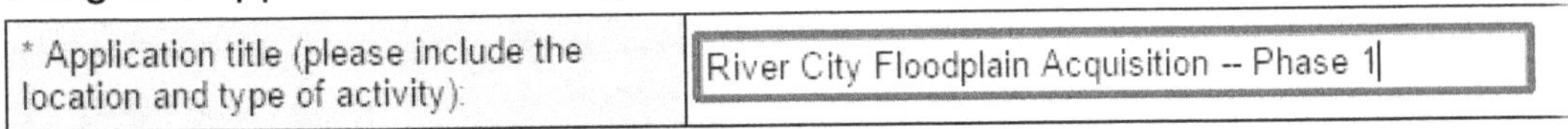

To begin a new subapplication, select the **Create New Application** link on the Subgrant Applicant Home Page.

* Application title (please include the location and type of activity):	River City Floodplain Acquisition -- Phase 1

The first part of creating a subapplication is to give it a title. It is recommended that you include the location and type of activity in the title of the subapplication. Select the **Application Title** field. You need to enter the name of the River City subapplication. So, type "River City Floodplain Acquisition—Phase 1."

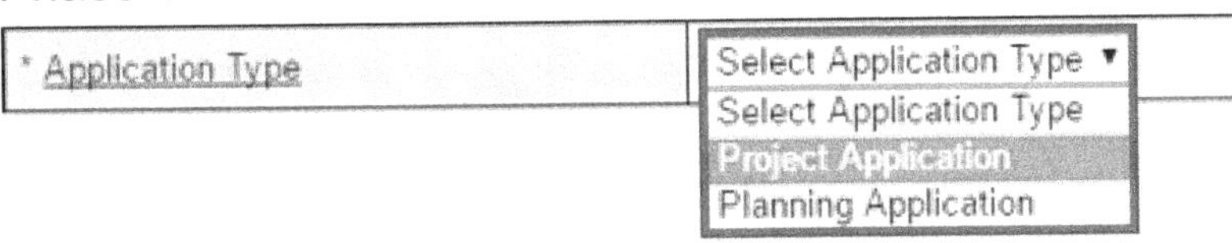

Select the **Application Type** drop-down menu. This drop-down menu has two options: Project Application or Planning Application. For our scenario, you need to select the option for "Project Application."

Select the **Save and Continue** button to save what we have entered for later retrieval. You have just created a new subapplication.

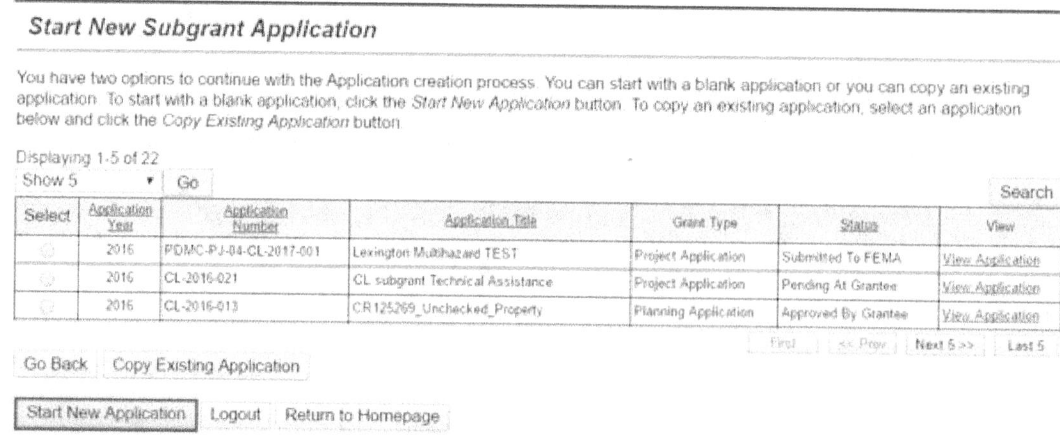

The Start New Subgrant Application screen appears. Select the **Start New Application** button at the bottom of the screen.

The Application Status screen appears. You can see all the sections of the project subapplication you will have to complete.

Copying an Existing Subapplication

You can also begin a new subapplication by copying an existing subapplication. The resulting copy will be either partially or completely filled with data from the original one, depending on which sections of the subapplication you selected to be copied and the status of each of those sections.

Note — In addition to copying information from an existing planning or project subapplications to a new subapplication, information from an existing pre-application can be copied to a new pre-application.

Note — If you choose to copy an entire subapplication, all of the attachments and comments associated with the existing subapplication will also be copied.

Copying an Existing Subapplication (continued)

In the slideshow below, Sally demonstrates how to copy an existing subapplication.
Scroll down to see slideshow captions.

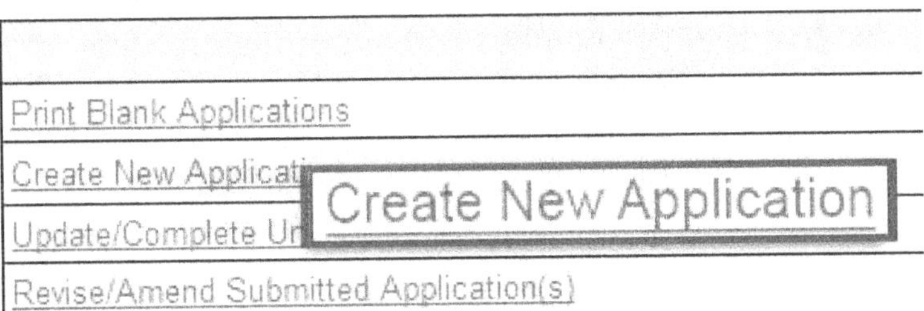

To create a new subgrant application by copying an existing subgrant application, select the **Create New Application** link on the Subgrant Applicant Home Page.

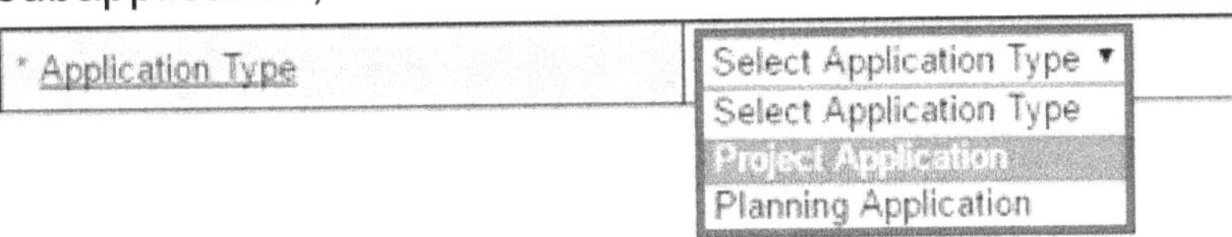

Like before, you first need to give your subapplication a title. Select the **Application Title** text box to enter the name of the subapplication. Type "River City Floodplain Acquisition—Phase 1," the name of the River City subapplication, in the text box.

Next, select the **Application Type** drop-down menu to see the options. We can choose between the two options: Project Application or Planning Application. We need to select the "Project Application" option for our subapplication.

Select the **Save and Continue** button to store the data we have just entered into eGrants so we can retrieve it later.

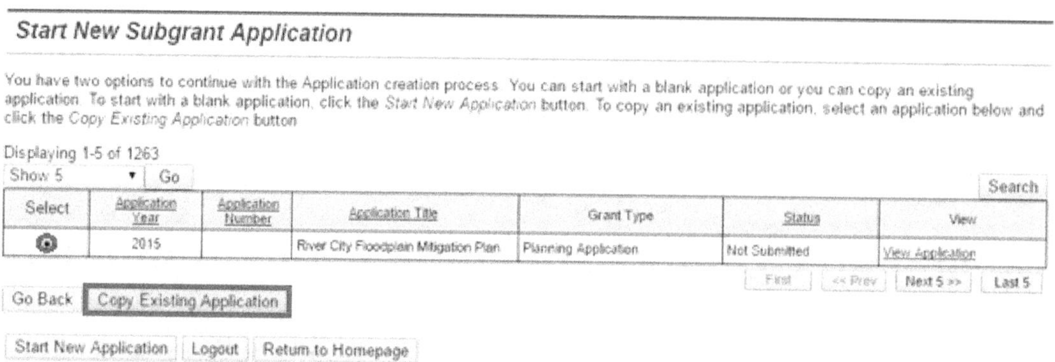

Next, you need to select the radio button in the **Select** column for the subapplication title you wish to copy. We want to copy information from another subapplication submitted by River City a few years ago. So we will select the radio button next to the 2015 River City Floodplain Mitigation Plan subapplication. Then, select the **Copy Existing Application** button.

Copy Subgrant Application Sections

Please select the sections you want to copy into the River City Floodplain Acquisition -- Phase 1 application. When you are finished, click the Save and Continue button below.

Select	Application Section
☑	Subapplicant
☐	Contact
☐	Community
☐	Mitigation Plan
☐	Schedule
☐	Scope of Work
☐	Cost Estimate
☐	Cost Share
☐	Evaluation
☐	Comments and Attachments
☐	FEMA Grants Application
☐	Comments for FEMA
☐	Entire Application

You can select either the checkbox in the **Select** column that corresponds to the section you wish to copy. Or you can select the checkbox for the "Entire

Application" option. Today, You just want to select the "Subapplicant" checkbox.

| Save and Continue |

Then select the **Save and Continue** button to save the copied Subapplicant section to our newly created subapplication in the eGrants system.

Copying Risks

When copying an existing subapplication, you need to be careful to avoid copying:

- **Outdated information:** Since the original subapplication was created in the past, some information may have changed. For example, contact information may have changed since the previous subapplication was created. Also, the grant program guidelines may have changed.
- **Irrelevant Information:** While the original subapplication may have been for a similar project, it's not safe for you to assume that *all* of the information in the previous subapplication will be appropriate for the new one.

It's always best to review every item in the subapplication for accuracy prior to submission. Furthermore, it's a good idea to review the grant program regulations and guidance to ensure all required and relevant information is provided in the subapplication.

Lesson 5 Summary

You've just completed the Creating Subapplications lesson. In this lesson, you learned that:

- Subapplicants must create a project pre-application, when requested by an Applicant
- Subapplicants may create project or planning subapplications
- To start a new, blank subapplication, you can select the Start New Application button from the Start New Subgrant Application screen
- To start a new subapplication populated with data previously entered in another subapplication, you can select the Copy Exiting Application button from the Start New Subgrant Application screen
- You should ensure that all information from a copied subapplication is current and relevant to the new subapplication

Lesson 6 Overview

Upon completion of this lesson, you should be able to:

- Identify the information collected in the different sections of Flood Mitigation Assistance (FMA) and Pre-Disaster Mitigation (PDM) subapplications

Acquisition Scenario

Name: Sally Watkins

Community: River City, State of Columbia

Problem: Repetitive flooding of three properties along the South Branch of the Washburn River

Proposed Solution: To acquire and demolish the properties and replace them with a community park

To Date: You created a subapplication but haven't had a chance to enter any information into it.

Your Next Step: You need to explore a subapplication and learn how to complete the different sections.

Listen to Sally
Audio transcript

Hello. It's Sally again. Last week we created a Flood Mitigation Assistance project subapplication. I know you haven't had a chance to complete it. Before you start entering data into the subapplication, I think it is important to take a look at its different sections. To do this, we first need to find the subapplication in eGrants.

Subapplication Sections

A subapplication contains many sections. While planning and project subapplications have a few of the same sections, most of them are different.

The sections of a subapplication can be accessed using the sidebar menu, as shown in the example sections of a project subapplication on the right side of the screen. The sections also appear in the Application Status screen when a new subapplication is created. All sections of a subapplication must be completed before it can be successfully submitted to an Applicant.

Preview all the sections of a project subapplication to become familiar with the information requirements. **Select each of the numbered links** in the sidebar menu to the right to view the information requirements. **Click on the image** displayed to view a dialog box that provides important details about that section.

After you look through the information required, Sally will demonstrate how to complete all of the subapplication sections.

Application Status

1.Application Status
2.Subapplicant
3.Contact
4.Community
5.Mitigation Plan
6.Scope of Work
7.Properties
8.Schedule
9.Cost Estimate
10.Cost Share
11.Cost Effectiveness
12.Environmental/Historic Preservation
13.Evaluation
14.Assurances and Certifications
15.Comments and Attachments
16.Review and Submit Application

Print Application
Return to Home Page
Logout
Privacy Statement
Disclaimers

Click on each numbered link on this sidebar menu to access information about the subapplication sections.

Select this link for a full description of the image.
Click on the image for more information.

Application Status

This screen shows the Status of the different sections of the full application. If the Status is Incomplete, you may click on the link to complete that section or you may use the menu on the left

Application Section	Status
Subapplicant	Incomplete
Contact	Incomplete
Community	Incomplete
Mitigation Plan	Incomplete
Scope of Work	Incomplete
Properties	Incomplete
Schedule	Incomplete
Cost Estimate	Incomplete
Cost Share	Incomplete
Cost Effectiveness	Incomplete
Environmental/Historic Preservation	Incomplete
Evaluation	Incomplete
Assurances and Certifications	Incomplete
Comments and Attachments	Complete
Comments for FEMA	Incomplete

Select this link for the full text of the image.

Application Status

You can use this page to monitor your progress toward completing the subapplication. It is also a quick way move between sections by selecting the status link located beside the section on which you would like to work.

Click on the image for more information.

Select this link for the full text of the image.

Subapplicant Section

This section is used to collect information necessary to identify the Subgrant Applicant. You can **search** for the organization using the Find Organization button, and much of the information will be added automatically. If you need an explanation of any of the fields, select the hyperlinks or **Help** links associated with those fields.

Click on the image for more information.

Contact

Please provide the following information. When you are finished, click the *Save and Continue* button below.

Note: Fields marked with an * are required. The address of the Point of Contact should be the Agency/Organization address applying for FEMA funds.

Authorized Subgrant Agent		Contact POC Help
Title	Mr. ▼	
* First Name		
Middle Initial		
* Last Name		
Title		
* Agency/Organization		Find Organization
* Address 1		
Address 2		
* City		
* State	Kentucky ▼	
* ZIP	- (e.g. 70354-4456)	Need help for ZIP+4?
* Phone	(e.g. 703-456-7890) Ext.	
Fax	(e.g. 703-457-7890)	
* Email	(e.g. user@xyz.org)	Contact eMail Help

To add a Point of Contact, please complete all the information below.

Point of Contact		
Title	Mr. ▼	
* First Name		
Middle Initial		
* Last Name		
Title		
* Agency/Organization		Find Organization
* Address 1		
Address 2		
* City		
* State	Choose ▼	
* ZIP	- (e.g. 70354-4456)	Need help for ZIP+4?
* Phone	(e.g. 703-456-7890) Ext.	
Fax	(e.g. 703-457-7890)	
* Email	(e.g. user@xyz.org)	Contact eMail Help

Select this link for the full text of the image.

Contact Section

This section is used to collect contact information about personnel within the Subgrant Applicant organization, or the Grant Applicant organization acting as a Subgrant Applicant. You need to provide information for both the authorized agent and a Point of Contact (POC). The **Help** links provide information to help you complete the section.

Click on the image for more information.

Community

Please provide the following information. When you are finished, click the *Save and Continue* button below.
In case the Congressional district number for your community is not showing up correctly then please contact your State NFIP coordinator.

Note: Fields marked with an * are required.

Please find the community(ies) that will benefit from this mitigation activity by clicking on the Find Community button. You shall modify Congressional District for each community by directly editing the textbox(es) provided. You should also notify your State NFIP coordinator so that it can be updated in the Community Information System database. When you are finished, click the *Save and Continue* button below.

*	Find Community								
(If the benefit is statewide, the applicant should select "Statewide" in the community listing)									
County Code	Community Name	CID Number	CRS Community	CRS Rating	State Legislative District	US Congressional District	State	Action	

If you would like to make any comments, please enter them below.

(Maximum 4000 characters)

To attach documents, click the *Attach File* button below.

Attach File

Find Community

You may search for a community by entering the following information. When you are finished, click the *Search* button.

State	CL
Community Name	
County Name	
Sort by	Community Name ▼
Results per page	Community Name
	County Code
	CID Number
	CRS Community
	CRS Rating
	US Congressional District

Go Back   Search

Select this link for the full text of the image.

Community section

The Community section is used to collect information about the community that will benefit from the federal subaward. You can search for information on a community by clicking the Find Community button. We will learn more about this section later in this lesson.

Click on the image for more information.

Mitigation Plan

Please provide your plan information below. If you have already submitted a plan, you may search the FEMA Plans Repository by clicking the *Find Plan* button. When you are finished, click the *Save and Continue* button below.

Note: Fields marked with an * are required.

* Is the entity that will benefit from the proposed activity covered by a current FEMA-approved multihazard mitigation plan in compliance with 44 CFR Part 201?	Yes ○ No ○ Not Known ○

If Yes, please answer the following:

If your plan is on file with FEMA you can search for it and attach it electronically. To begin your search in the Plans Repository , click Find Plan. `[Find Plan]`

* What is the name of the plan?	
* What is the type of plan?	▼
* When was the current multihazard mitigation plan approved by FEMA?	(MM-DD-YYYY e.g. 02-05-2002)
* Describe how the proposed activity relates to or is consistent with the FEMA-approved mitigation plan.	(Maximum 4000 characters)

If No or Not Known, please answer the following:

* Does the entity have any other mitigation plans adopted?	Yes ○ No ○ Not Known ○

If Yes, please provide plan information by clicking the *Add Plan* button.

Plan Name	Plan Type	Date Adopted	Attachment	Action

`[Add Plan]`

* Does the State/Tribe in which the entity is located have a current FEMA-approved mitigation plan in compliance with 44 CFR Part 201?	Yes ○ No ○

If Yes, please answer the following:

If your plan is on file with FEMA you can search for it and attach it electronically. To begin your search in the Plans Repository , click Find Plan. `[Find Plan]`

* What is the name of the plan?	
* What is the type of plan?	▼
* When was the current multihazard mitigation plan approved by FEMA?	(MM-DD-YYYY e.g. 02-05-2003)
* Describe how the proposed activity relates to or is consistent with the State/Tribe's FEMA-approved mitigation plan.	Help (Maximum 4000 characters)

If you would like to make any comments, please enter them below.

(Maximum 4000 characters)

To attach documents, click the *Attach File* button below.

`[Attach File]`

Select this link for the full text of the image.

Mitigation Plan Section

This is where you provide information about our FEMA-approved hazard mitigation plan. You can search for a previously submitted mitigation plan in the FEMA Plans Repository by selecting the Find Plan button.

Click on the image for more information.

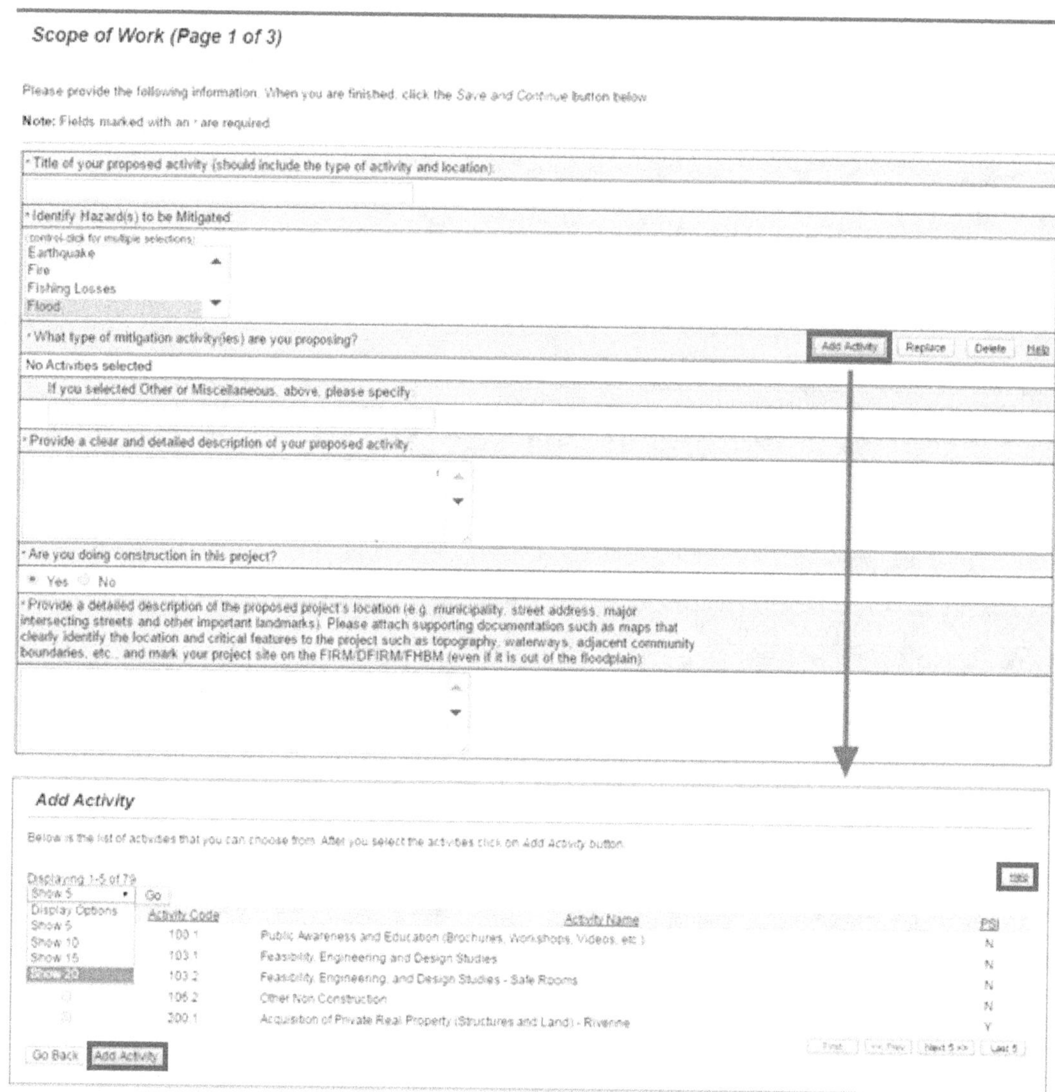

Select this link for the full text of the image.

Scope of Work Section

This is where you provide detailed information about the mitigation activity proposed in our subapplication.

There are three parts to the Scope of Work section. Part 1 asks for the name, type of hazard to be mitigated, type(s) of mitigation activity(ies) proposed, and a description of the location of the affected area. **For Flood Mitigation Assistance subapplications, it is important to specify "Flood" as the primary type of hazard to be mitigated.**

Part 2 asks for latitude and longitude for the project area; an explanation for the need for the activity, who it will benefit, and how the activity will be implemented; and information on the project manager and contractors for the project. In addition, details on the technical feasibility of the project are required.

Part 3 asks for information on how the project will address the identified hazard and any residual risks that will remain after completion of the project. It also asks for information on when the activity will take place, why the activity was selected from other alternative solutions, and information on long-term maintenance that will be provided for the area impacted.

We will learn how to complete Part 1 of the Scope of Work section later in this lesson.

Click on the image for more information.

Properties (Page 1 of 4)

This section will enable you to add properties to be mitigated. To add a property, click the *Add Property* button below. To update or delete a property already added to your project, click the appropriate link under the *Action* column. Depending on the activity you selected from the *Scope Of Work* section, some activities may require additional information and some may not. If you do not want to add additional property information for an activity that has the option to, check the *Property Information Not Applicable* checkbox. When you are finished, click the *Save and Continue* button below.

Note: Fields marked with an * are required. Properties marked with an ** are incomplete.

Acquisition of Public Real Property (Structures and Land) - Riverine (200.3)								
Property Owner's Name	Address of Property to be Mitigated	City	ZIP	NFIP	Policy #	FMA Repetitive Loss	FMA Severe Repetitive Loss	Property Locator #	Action

* Add Property | Import Property

Select this link for the full text of the image.

Properties Section

This is where you add information about the properties that will be affected by your project. You can manually add property information by selecting the Add Property button.

You can also add multiple properties at one time by selecting the Import Property button and uploading an Excel spreadsheet with the property information. You can download a sample Excel file by using the link within the Import Properties screen. You must add properties for each proposed activity. You must complete all four pages of the Properties Section to successfully submit your subapplication.

For Flood Mitigation Assistance subapplications, it is necessary to provide the **National Flood Insurance Program (NFIP) policy number** for each property listed.

Click on the image for more information.

Schedule

Enter Work Schedule
Please include all tasks necessary to implement this mitigation activity, the estimated timeframe for each task, and who will complete it.

Add Task

* Estimate the total duration of the proposed activity:
(Must equal or exceed each task duration)

[   ] Day(s) ▼

Add Task

Please provide the following information. When you are finished, click the *Save and Continue* button below.

Note: Fields marked with an * are required

* Description of Task			
			(e.g. Ordering Shutters.)
* Starting Point	Unit Of Time	* Duration	Unit Of Time
(start day of the task e.g. 4)	Day(s) ▼ (e.g. Days)	(a number e.g. 3)	Day(s) ▼ (e.g. Days)
Who will complete the work?			

Select this link for the full text of the image.

Schedule Section

This section is where you add information about each task necessary to complete the mitigation activity you're proposing in your subapplication. **Click on the image for more information.**

<u>Select this link for the full text of the image.</u>

Cost Estimate section

The Cost Estimate section is for identifying the details of budgeted items described in the Scope of Work section. All costs must be based on industry standards. Note that maintenance costs are not included. Select the Add Item button to open a new screen to document estimated costs for elements listed in your proposed Scope of Work. We will learn more about this section later in this lesson.

Click on the image for more information.

Cost Share

The Cost Share is automatically calculated to 75% Federal / 25% non-Federal. If you modify the Non-Federal Share amount, click the Recalculate Share button to compute the new Federal and Non-Federal Share Percentages.

Please provide the following information. When you are finished, click the *Save and Continue* button below. Please add the funding source records whose total amount should be greater than or equal to the proposed non-Federal share amount.

Note: Fields marked with an * are required.

Please correct the following error(s) before proceeding:

- Please complete Cost Estimate section before filling in the Cost Share details.

	Dollars	Percentage
Activity Cost Estimate (If you modify the Federal Share Percentage or Non-Federal Share amount, click the Recalculate Share button to compute the new Federal Share.)	$ 0.00	
Federal Share Percentage	75%	Help
Non-Federal Share Percentage	25%	Help
* Proposed Federal Share (Calculated based on the Federal Share Percentage) Notes: for L-PDM grants, Federal Share may be up to 90% for small, impoverished community.	$ 0.00	75%
*Proposed Non-Federal Share (Calculated based on the Non-Federal Share Percentage)	$ 0.00	25% Recalculate Share

Non-Federal Funds

Please add your non-Federal funds below by clicking the *Add Cost Share* button. To update or delete funds click the appropriate link under the *Action* column.

* Add Cost Share

Source Agency	Name of Source Agency	Funding Type	Amount ($)	Action
			Grand Total	$ 0.00

If you would like to make any comments, please enter them below.

(Maximum 4000 characters)

To attach documents, click the *Attach File* button below.

Attach File

(You will be able to add attachments, once this form is saved.)

Select this link for the full text of the image.

Cost Share section

After the Cost Estimate section is complete, you use the Cost Share section to calculate the federal and non-federal share of the estimated costs and to document your funding sources. We will learn more about this section later in this lesson.

Click on the image for more information.

Cost Effectiveness

Please provide the following information. Cost Effectiveness is based on the **entire project**. When complete, click the *Save and Continue* button below to continue to the next section.

Note: Fields marked with an * are required. All Projects require Cost Effectiveness data. Please see the Benefit Cost web page for more information.

Attach the Benefit Cost Analysis (BCA), if completed for this project.

Name	Date Attached	Action

Attach

* Net Present Value of Project Benefits (A)	$
* Total Project Cost Estimate (B) (Note: The Total Project Cost from the Benefit Cost Analysis (BCA) should be entered here vs. the total from the Cost Estimate section of this application, as maintenance costs are not eligible for grant funding but are considered in the BCA.)	$
* What is the Benefit Cost Ratio for the entire project (A/B)?	

If you would like to make any comments, please enter them below.

(Maximum 4000 characters)

To attach documents, click the *Attach File* button below.

Attach File

Select this link for the full text of the image.

Cost Effectiveness section

The Cost Effectiveness section collects information about the cost effectiveness of the proposed mitigation activity. The information to be provided here is based on a FEMA-approved Benefit-Cost Analysis. This section documents your analysis of the expected benefits and the estimated total cost of the proposed mitigation project or mitigation plan. **Maintenance costs are included in the Benefit-Cost Analysis, so it is important to use the Total Project Costs figures generated through that analysis when completing this section.**

For planning subapplications, none of the fields in this section is required. Therefore, when you first start the subapplication, the status of this section will be identified as "Complete."

Click on the image for more information.

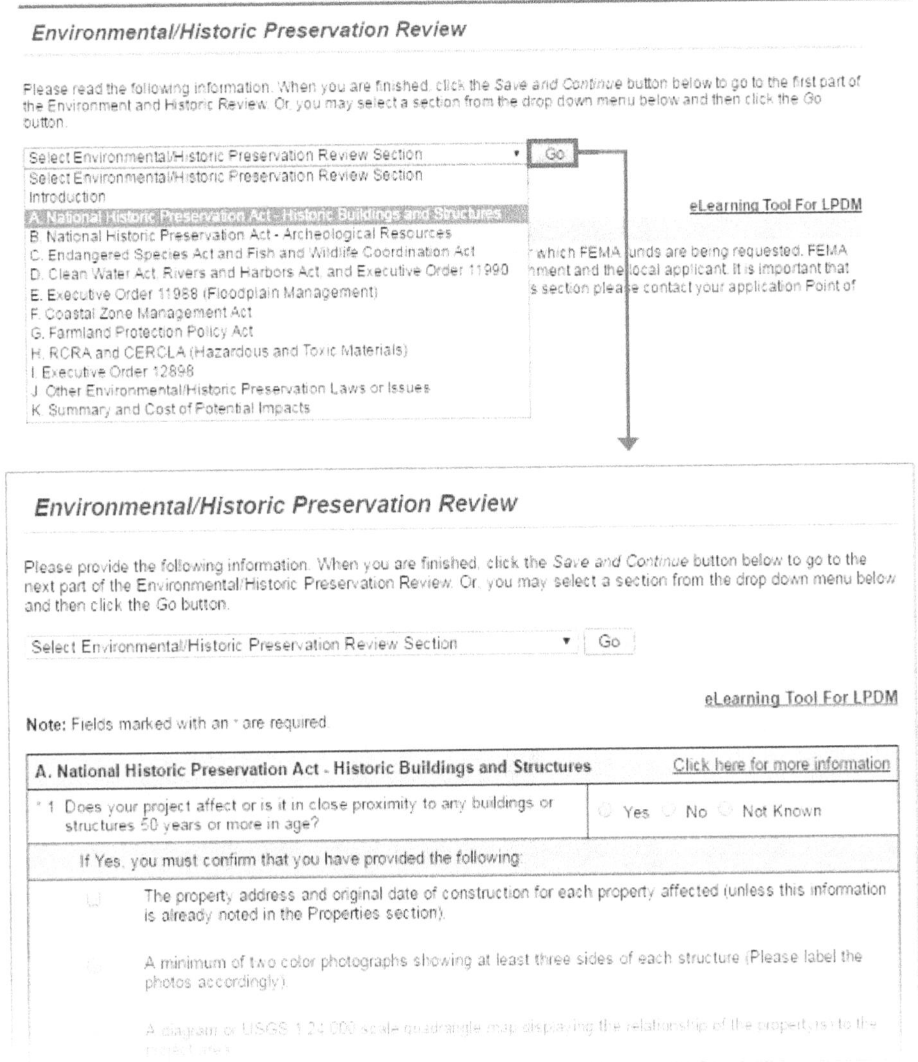

[Select this link for the full text of the image.](#)

Environmental/Historical Preservation Review section

This section gathers information on your proposed mitigation project in terms of 11 different environmental and historic preservation laws and executive orders. Most planning subapplications qualify for a Categorical Exclusion (CATEX). However, **project Subapplicants must answer questions in all sections. Click on the image for more information.**

Evaluation

Please click the link below to complete or modify the different parts of the *Evaluation Information* section. If the section is not applicable, check the *Not Applicable* box provided below. When you are finished, click the *Save and Continue* button.

By checking the Not Applicable box and not providing the information in this section, I understand that this application may not be selected for the Pre-Disaster Mitigation - Competitive Grant Program (PDMC) nor Legislative Pre-Disaster Mitigation Program (LPDM).

Incomplete   ☐ Not applicable

Evaluation (Page 1 of 2)

Please provide the following information. When you are finished, click the *Save and Continue* button below.

Note: Fields marked with an * are required.

		Help
* Is the recipient participating in the Community Rating System (CRS)?	○ Yes ○ No	Help
If yes, what is their CRS rating?	▾	
* Is the recipient a Cooperating Technical Partner (CTP)?	○ Yes ○ No	Help
* Is the recipient a Firewise Community?	○ Yes ○ No	Help
If yes, please provide their Firewise Community number.		
* Has the recipient adopted building codes consistent with the International Codes?	○ Yes ○ No	Help
* Has the recipient adopted the National Fire Protection Association (NFPA) 5000 Code?	○ Yes ○ No	Help
* Have the recipient's building codes been assessed on the Building Code Effectiveness Grading Schedule (BCEGS)?	○ Yes ○ No	Help
If yes, what is their BCEGS rating?	▾	
* Is this a small, impoverished community?	○ Yes ○ No	Help

Select this link for the full text of the image.

Evaluation section

A Subapplicant must complete this section if applying to the Pre-Disaster Mitigation program. Detailed information about the proposed project or mitigation plan must be provided, which will be used by the Applicant to rank subapplications within an application. If a Subapplicant is applying to the FMA program, the "Not Applicable" box can be checked.

Click on the image for more information.

Forms	Status
Part I. Assurances Non-Construction Programs.	Incomplete
	☐ Not Applicable
Part II. Certifications Regarding Lobbying; Debarment, Suspension and Other Responsibilities Matters; and Drug-Free Workplace Requirements.	Incomplete
Part III. SF-LLL, Disclosure of Lobbying Activities (Complete only if applying for a grant of more than $100,000 and have lobbying activities using Non-Federal funds. See the Certifications Regarding Lobbying; Debarment, Suspension and Other Responsibilities Matters; and Drug-Free Workplace Requirements form for lobbying activities definition.)	Incomplete
	☐ Not Applicable

Select this link for the full text of the image.

Assurances and Certifications section

This link will only be available if your Grant Applicant requires Assurances and Certifications for your subgrant application. The Assurances and Certifications section provides documents listing Federal requirements for FEMA grants. There are four documents that may appear in this section. We will learn more about this section later in this lesson.

Click on the image for more information.

Comments and Attachments

This section will enable you to add comments or attach files to supplement any section you have already completed. To add a comment or attachment, click on the *Add* button. You may also update or delete any comments. To update or delete a comment, click on the link in the *Action* column.

Name of Section	Comment	Attachment	Date Attached	Action
Add				

Add Comments and Attachments

You may enter your new comments in the box below, or you may include additional information as an attachment. Please be sure to provide the name of the section to which your comment or attachment refers.

Name of section:

Application Level ▼

If you would like to make any comments, please enter them below.

(Maximum 4000 characters)

To attach documents, click the *Attachments* button below. (You may include Photographs; Property deed; Tax assessment; Tax parcel map; Flood Insurance Rate Map (FIRM) with project site marked; Insurance settlements/documentation; Engineering or design specifications; etc.)

Name	Date Attached	Action

Attachments

<u>Select this link for the full text of the image.</u>

Comments and Attachments section

The Comments and Attachments section displays all the comments entered for and documents that have been attached to your subapplication for easy review. You can also use this section to attach additional electronic files or indicate that you are sending supporting document via regular mail. To facilitate the review of the subapplication by the Applicant and FEMA reviewers, it is best to add comments and attachments directly to the section they concern. We will learn more about this section later in this lesson.

Click on the image for more information.

Each section of your application to your grant applicant is listed below. If any required information is missing from a section, its status will be listed as incomplete. You can return to that section of the application by clicking the incomplete link. Once all sections of your Application are **complete**, you may submit your application. To submit the application you should have the correct authentication.

Note: Fields marked with an * are required.

Print

Select	Application Section	Status
	Subapplicant	Complete
	Contact	Incomplete
	Community	Complete
	Mitigation Plan	Complete
	Scope of Work	Incomplete
	Properties	Incomplete
	Schedule	Incomplete
	Cost Estimate	Incomplete
	Cost Share	Complete
	Cost Effectiveness	Complete
	Environmental/Historic Preservation	Incomplete
	Evaluation	Complete
	Assurances and Certifications	Incomplete
	Comments and Attachments	Complete
	FEMA Grants Application	Incomplete
	Entire Application	Incomplete

<u>Select this link for the full text of the image.</u>

Review and Submit Subgrant Application section

Using this section, you can review the completion status of each section of your subapplication. All sections must have a status of "Complete" before the subapplication can be successfully submitted to the Applicant. We will learn more about this section later in this lesson.

Subapplicant Section

The Subapplicant section will appear for all types of subapplications. A complete Subapplicant section will contain detailed information about the organization requesting the subaward. The information includes type of Subapplicant, tax number, and Federal Employer Identification Number (EIN). The fields that are marked with an asterisk (*) are required, while the remainder are optional.

Sally will help you complete the Subapplicant section of the River City Floodplain Acquisition—Phase 1 subapplication. She will provide you with the appropriate information for the screens as you need it. River City is the name of the Subapplicant.

Scroll down to see slideshow captions.

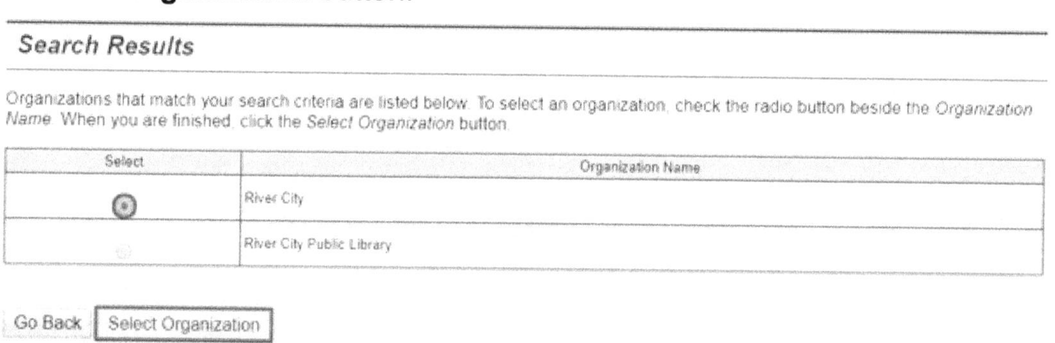

To help you complete parts of the Subapplicant section, there are features built into eGrants that provide information. The first one is the **Find Organization** button. We use this to make sure that the name of the Subapplicant is consistent throughout eGrants. You need to enter the first few letters of the Subapplicant's name in the text field. In our case, River City is applying for a subaward. So, type "River" in the **Name of Subapplicant** text field and select the **Find Organization** button.

The Search Results screen appears and displays a list of organizations. Select the radio button in the **Select** column next to the name River City. Then, select the **Select Organization** button. This inserts the name of the Subapplicant and the State field automatically into the Subapplicant section.

Name of Subapplicant	River City
	Find Organization
State	CL
Type of Subapplicant	Select Type ▼
	Select Type
	State Government
	Local Government
	Indian Tribal Government
	Special Governmental District
	Private Non-Profit
	Other

This inserts the name of the Subapplicant and the State automatically into the Subapplicant section. Select the **Type of Subapplicant** drop-down menu to display the types of Subapplicants. This drop-down menu has six options. We need to choose the appropriate Subapplicant type. In our case, we should select the "Local Government" option. At this point, you can scroll down and complete the other fields on this screen.

Contact Section

The Contact section collects information about whom to contact if there are questions about the subapplication. The Contact section requires that contact information for an Authorized Subgrant Agent be provided such as name of the agent, name of the agency, address (i.e., of the agency/organization), phone number, and e-mail address.
A Point of Contact (POC) is not required, but is suggested. Both the POC and the Authorized Subgrant Agent may be notified via e-mail by the Applicant regarding the status of the subapplication once it has been submitted.

Contact

Please provide the following information. When you are finished, click the *Save and Continue* button below.

Note: Fields marked with an * are required. The address of the Point of Contact should be the Agency/Organization address applying for FEMA funds.

Authorized Subgrant Agent		Contact POC Help
Title	Mr. ▼	
* First Name		
Middle Initial		
* Last Name		
Title		
* Agency/Organization		Find Organization
* Address 1		
Address 2		
* City		
* State	Kentucky ▼	
* ZIP	- (e.g. 70354-4456) Need help for ZIP+4?	
* Phone	(e.g. 703-456-7890) Ext.	
Fax	(e.g. 703-457-7890)	
* Email	(e.g. user@xyz.org) Contact eMail Help	

To add a Point of Contact, please complete all the information below.

Point of Contact		
Title	Mr. ▼	
* First Name		
Middle Initial		
* Last Name		
Title		
* Agency/Organization		Find Organization
* Address 1		
Address 2		
* City		
* State	Choose ▼	
* ZIP	- (e.g. 70354-4456) Need help for ZIP+4?	
* Phone	(e.g. 703-456-7890) Ext.	
Fax	(e.g. 703-457-7890)	
* Email	(e.g. user@xyz.org) Contact eMail Help	

<u>Select this link for the full text of the image.</u>

Community Section

Subapplicants must provide information about each community that will benefit from the subaward funds. This information will help the Applicant summarize information in its application.

Subapplicants should include information defining the project area in the Community Profile field in this section. The project area information will include details such as descriptions of the general population, special populations, significant industries, and businesses.

Sally is ready to show you how to work on the Community section of the River City subapplication.

Scroll down to see slideshow captions.

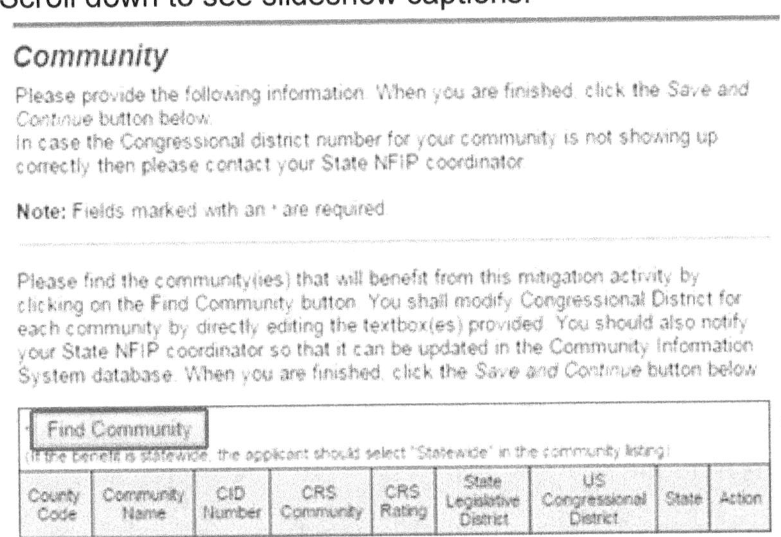

When you select the **Community** link on the sidebar menu, the Community section screen appears. From here, select the **Find Community** button.

To search for information about River City, you can complete either the **Community Name** or **County Name** field. You don't need to do both. You also don't need to type the entire name. eGrants can start a search using only a single letter. However, that can produce an undesirably long list of results. Today, just type "Rive" into the **Community Name** text field.

State	CL
Community Name	Rive
County Name	
Sort by	Community Name ▾
	Community Name
	County Code
	CID Number
	CRS Community
	CRS Rating
	US Congressional District
Results per page	

Go Back   Search

Next, select the **Sort By** drop-down menu. eGrants can sort the results by six different criteria. Select the "Community Name" option.

State	CL
Community Name	Rive
County Name	
Sort by	Community Name ▾
Results per page	20 ▾
	5
	10
	15
	20

Go Back   Search

Then, select the **Results per page** drop-down menu. This lets you determine how many search results will appear on each page. Select the "20" option. Finally, select the **Search** button.

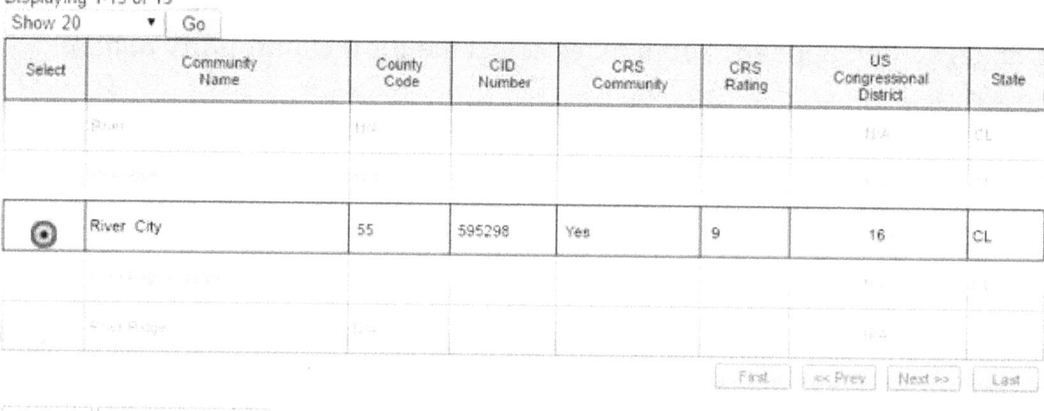

Communities that match your search criteria are listed below. To select a community, check the radio button beside the Community Name. When you are finished, click the Select Community button.

Displaying 1-13 of 13

Show 20   ▾   Go

Select	Community Name	County Code	CID Number	CRS Community	CRS Rating	US Congressional District	State
	River	N/A				N/A	CL
⦿	River City	55	595298	Yes	9	16	CL
	River Ridge	N/A				N/A	CL

First   << Prev   Next >>   Last

Go Back   Select Community

When the list of results appears, you'll want to select the radio button in the **Select** column on the left side of the community name you desire. We want to select the "River City" option.

Find Community								
County Code	Community Name	CID Number	CRS Community	CRS Rating	State Legislative District	US Congressional District	State	Action
55	River City	595298	Y	9	11	16	CL	Delete
N/A	River					N/A	CL	Delete

You see River City's name appear on the Community screen. Now you can scroll down and complete other fields on the screen.

Mitigation Plan Section

There are two parts to the Mitigation Plan section of the subapplication. The first section is where the Subapplicant provides the status of the local, state, or tribal mitigation plan under which it is covered. The second section asks for details on the status of the Applicant's state or tribal mitigation plan. Subapplicants must complete both sections.
If there is a FEMA-approved mitigation plan in compliance with Title 44, Code of Federal Regulations (CFR), Part 201 on file with FEMA, eGrants users can use the Find Plan button to locate the electronic copy of the plan in FEMA's Plan Repository, and the system will auto-fill the plan information in this section. If the mitigation plan is not in the Plan Repository, the Subapplicant should enter the name, type, and approval date of the plan. For project subapplications, the Subapplicant must describe how the proposed activity relates to or is consistent with the local, state, or tribal mitigation plan under which it is covered as well as the status of the Applicant's mitigation plan.

If any other mitigation plan has been adopted, the Subapplicant should provide information on that plan by selecting the Add Plan button.

Mitigation Plan Section (Continued)

Sally will show you how to complete the top portion of the Mitigation Plan section for the River City Floodplains Acquisition—Phase 1 subapplication.

Scroll down to see slideshow captions.

From the Application Status page, select the **Incomplete** link in the Status column on the right of the Mitigation Plan section.

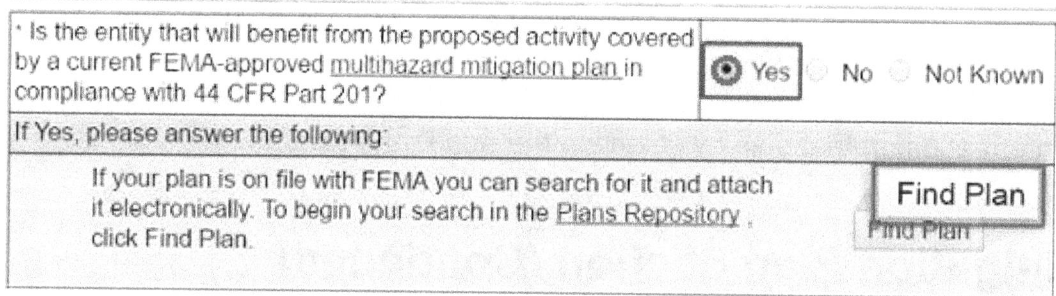

You can select the **radio button** on the left of the Yes, No, or Not Known options to indicate whether the community that will benefit from the proposed activity is covered by a current FEMA-approved multihazard mitigation plan. River City is covered, so select the **Yes** radio button. Since the River City plan is on file with FEMA, you can search for it and have the plan information automatically added to the form. To begin your search, select the **Find Plan** button.

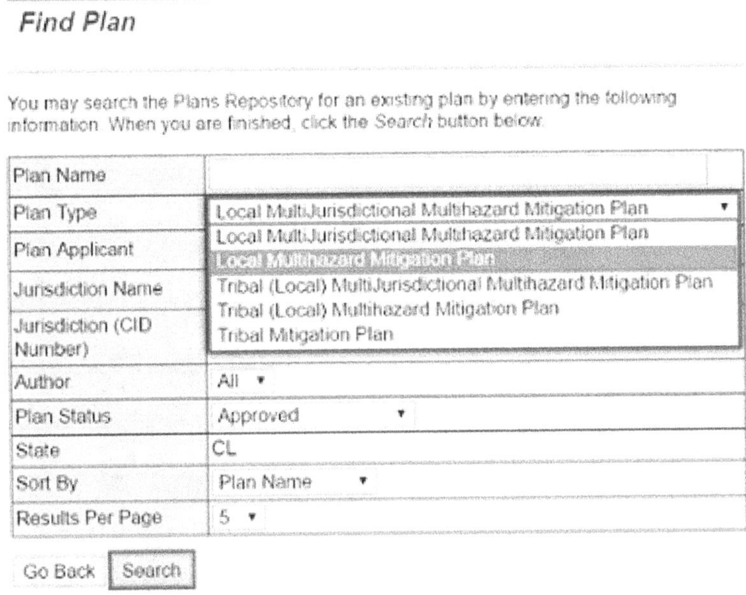

The Find Plan screen appears. You can search the Plans Repository by entering and sorting by the following criteria: Plan Name, Plan Type, Plan Applicant, Jurisdiction Name, CID Number, Author, and Plan Status. For the River City plan, select the **Plan Type** drop-down menu. This drop-down menu has five options. You need to select the "Local Multihazard Mitigation Plan." Then, select the **Search** button.

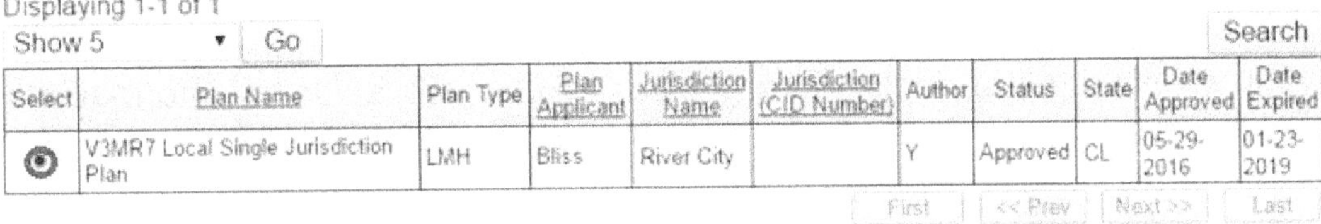

Select	Plan Name	Plan Type	Plan Applicant	Jurisdiction Name	Jurisdiction (CID Number)	Author	Status	State	Date Approved	Date Expired
◉	V3MR7 Local Single Jurisdiction Plan	LMH	Bliss	River City		Y	Approved	CL	05-29-2016	01-23-2019

Plans that match our search are listed. Select the radio button in the **Select** column that corresponds with the River City local single jurisdiction plan. Then, select the **Select Plan** button.

The following is a reproduced form:

* Is the entity that will benefit from the proposed activity covered by a current FEMA-approved multihazard mitigation plan in compliance with 44 CFR Part 201?	● Yes ○ No ○ Not Known

If Yes, please answer the following:

If your plan is on file with FEMA you can search for it and attach it electronically. To begin your search in the Plans Repository , click Find Plan. [Find Plan]

* What is the name of the plan?	V3MR7 Local Single Jurisdiction Plan
* What is the type of plan?	Local Multihazard Mitigation Plan ▼
* When was the current multihazard mitigation plan approved by FEMA?	05-29-2016 (MM-DD-YYYY e.g. 02-05-2002)
* Describe how the proposed activity relates to or is consistent with the FEMA-approved mitigation plan.	(Maximum 4000 characters) Section 1 describes the purpose and organization of the Plan Review Guide. Section 2 describes the overall guiding principles for Local Mitigation Plan reviews. Section 3 provides

You can see that the plan information is automatically populated from the plan you have selected. You now need to enter an **explanation** of how the proposed activity relates to or is consistent with the FEMA-approved mitigation plan in the text field.

[Save and Continue]

Then select the **Save and Continue** button.

Scope of Work Section

The Scope of Work section is for providing more detailed, specific information about the proposed mitigation activity, including a detailed description of the activity, its location, the method proposed to complete the activity, feasibility data, and identification of the contractors and project manager. This level of detail will provide the Applicant, as well as FEMA, with sufficient information to evaluate the proposed activity for effectiveness and eligibility for a subaward.

Note The information required for the Scope of Work section differs for planning, project, management costs, and technical assistance subapplications.

Complete the Scope of Work Section

Sally would like to show you how to complete the first part of the Scope of Work section for the River City Floodplain Acquisition—Phase 1 subapplication.
Scroll down to see slideshow captions.

The Scope of Work section has three parts. In the first part, we need to identify the types of mitigation activities proposed in the River City subapplication. From the **Identify Hazard(s) to be mitigated** drop-down menu, select the "Flood" option. Then, select the **Add Activity** button.

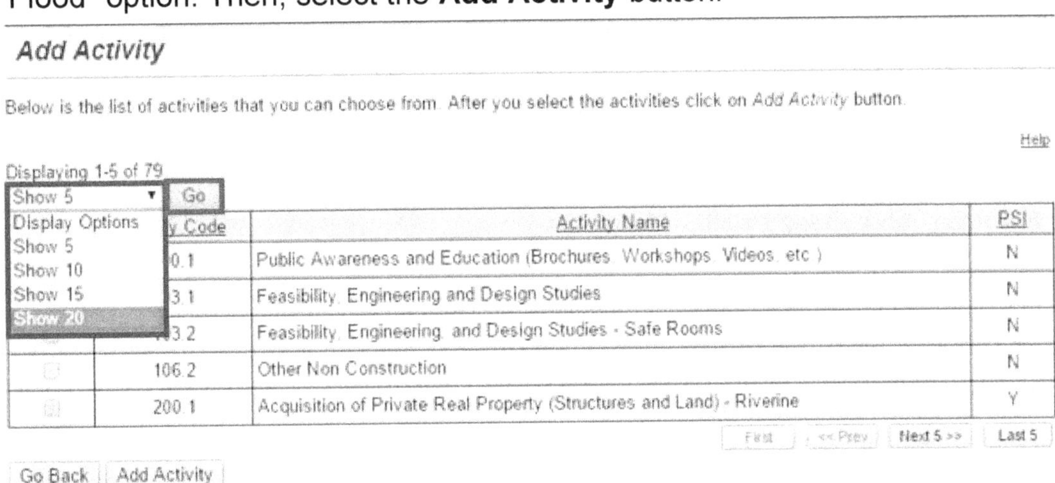

	y Code	Activity Name	PSI
	0.1	Public Awareness and Education (Brochures, Workshops, Videos, etc.)	N
	3.1	Feasibility, Engineering and Design Studies	N
	3.2	Feasibility, Engineering, and Design Studies - Safe Rooms	N
	106.2	Other Non Construction	N
	200.1	Acquisition of Private Real Property (Structures and Land) - Riverine	Y

We need to choose the activities proposed in the subapplication from the list provided. Select the **Display Options** drop-down menu to see up to 20 activities at once. Select the "Show 20" option so we can see a wide selection. Then, select the **Go** button.

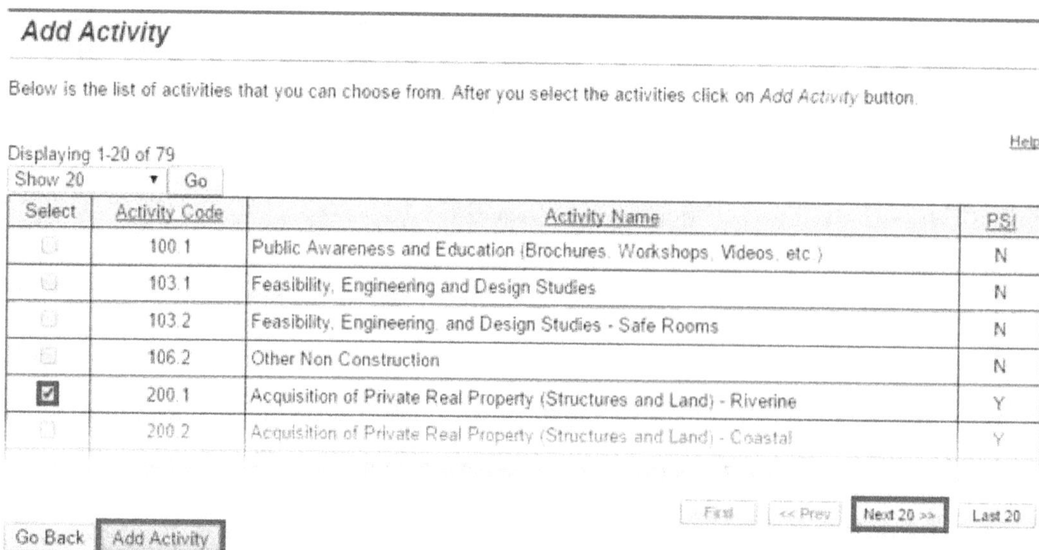

You can add multiple activities at the same time. You just select the checkboxes in the **Select** column to the left of the activity names and codes. Right now, select the checkbox next to "Activity Code 200.1" for acquisition of property near a riverine flooding area. To see more of the list of activities, select the **Next 20** button. Once we have selected the checkboxes for all of the activities we need to identify, select the **Add Activity** button.

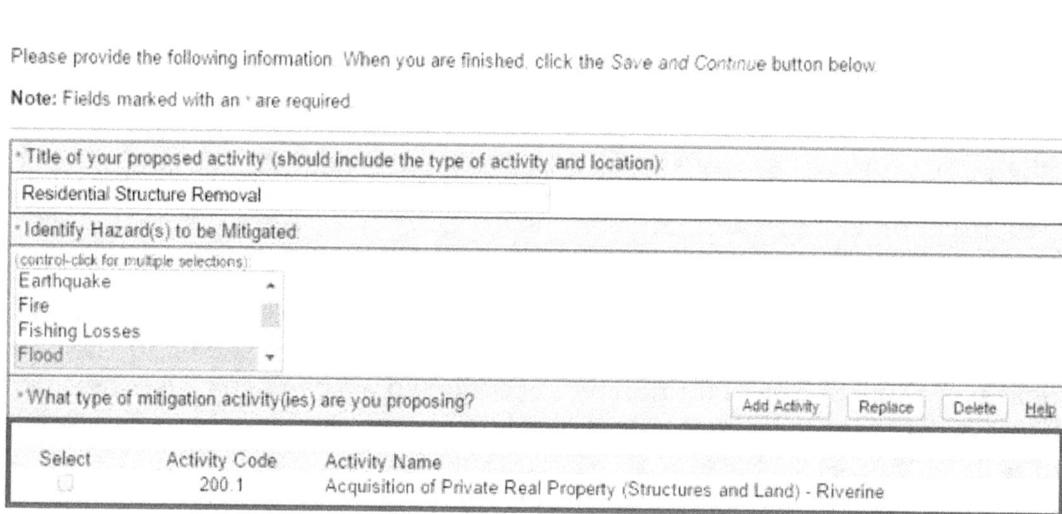

The activity that we added now appears on the list on the Scope of Work screen.

Save and Continue

You can repeat those steps to add more activities or select the **Save and Continue** button. That will save that information you just added and take you to Parts 2 and 3 of the Scope of Work section.

Properties Section

In a project subapplication, the Properties section allows the Subapplicant to designate the properties to be mitigated for each project activity selected in the Scope of Work section. Before you can add a property to the Properties section, you have to complete the Scope of Work section. Some of the types of activities selected in the Scope of Work will require property information and some will not. You must complete all four pages of the Properties Section to successfully submit your subapplication.

There are four steps to adding a property. First, select the Add Property button for an activity that will impact a property. Second, you will need to enter the property address and information about the owner and co-owner, if applicable. The last two parts of this section collect information about the property such as:

- Age and type of structure
- Purchase price
- Latitude and longitude
- Membership in National Flood Insurance Program (NFIP) and policy number
- Identification as a FMA Repetitive Loss property
- Identification as a FMA Severe Loss property
- Property Locator number
- Base Flood and First Floor Flood Elevations (if required)
- Property action

For FMA subapplications, it is necessary to provide the NFIP identification number for **all** properties.

This section is only required for project subapplications.

Note

You can also upload or import a list of properties from an Excel spreadsheet that will automatically populate the fields in the Add Property function.

Note

Schedule Section

The Schedule section is where you add detailed information about the length of time and sequence of each proposed activity listed In the Scope of Work section. You must list each task that is required to complete the activity, the expected timeframe, and when it should occur within the overall schedule for the activity. You are also required to provide information about the personnel who will perform each task.

Sally will show you how to add a task to the River City Floodplain Acquisition Project—Phase 1 schedule.

Scroll down to see slideshow captions.

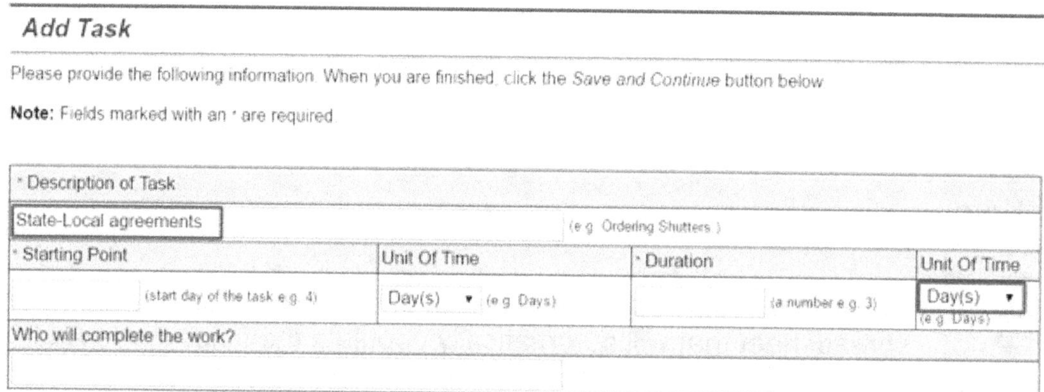

To add a task needed to complete the mitigation activity listed on the Scope of Work section of the River City Floodplain Acquisition—Phase 1 subapplication, select the **Add Task** button on the Schedule screen.

The Add Task screen appears. In the **Description of Task** text field you need to enter the name or a brief description of the task. Finalizing the agreements between River City and the State of Columbia is the first task that must be accomplished to begin the acquisition and demolition project. So, enter "State-Local agreements" in the Description of Task text field.

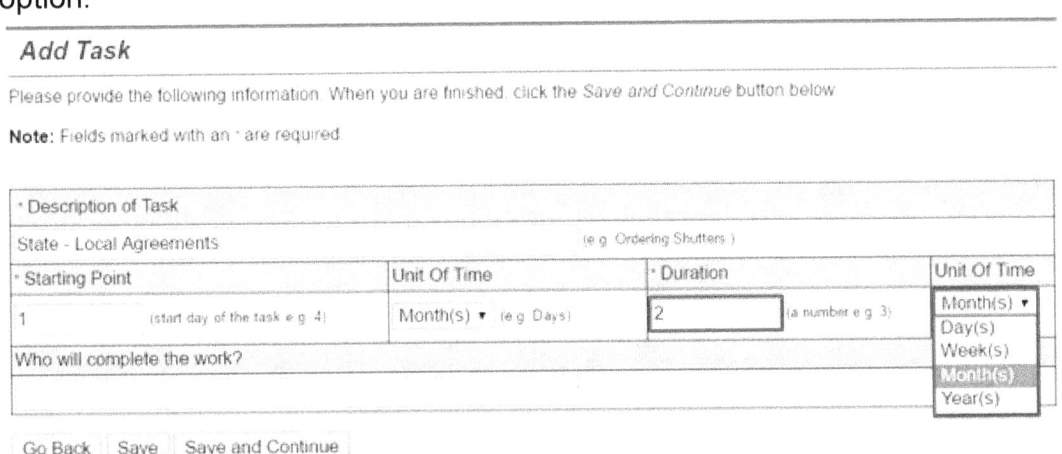

You must set a starting point for the mitigation project schedule. We will measure time for the project in months. In the **Starting Point** text field, enter "1." Then, using the **Unit of Time** drop-down menu, select the "Month(s)" option.

Now it is time to document how long it is estimated to accomplish the task. The project manager estimated that it will take about two months to complete the state-local agreements, so enter "2" in the **Duration** text field. Then, using the **Unit of Time** drop-down menu, select the "Month(s)" option.

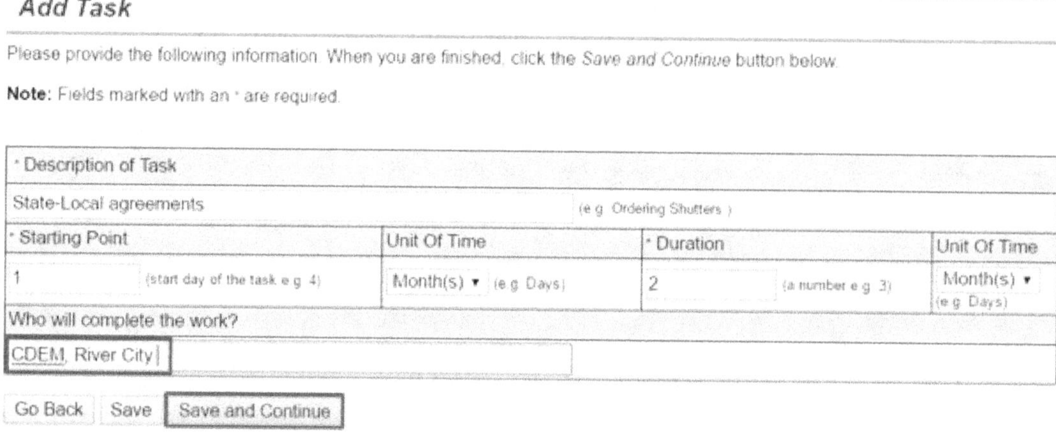

The Add Task screen asks: "Who will complete the work?" This is where you would enter the titles of individuals or companies responsible for completion of the task. For the State-Local Agreements task, the Columbia Department of Emergency Management and the River City local government will do the work. So, enter "CDEM, River City" in the text field. Then select the **Save and Continue** button.

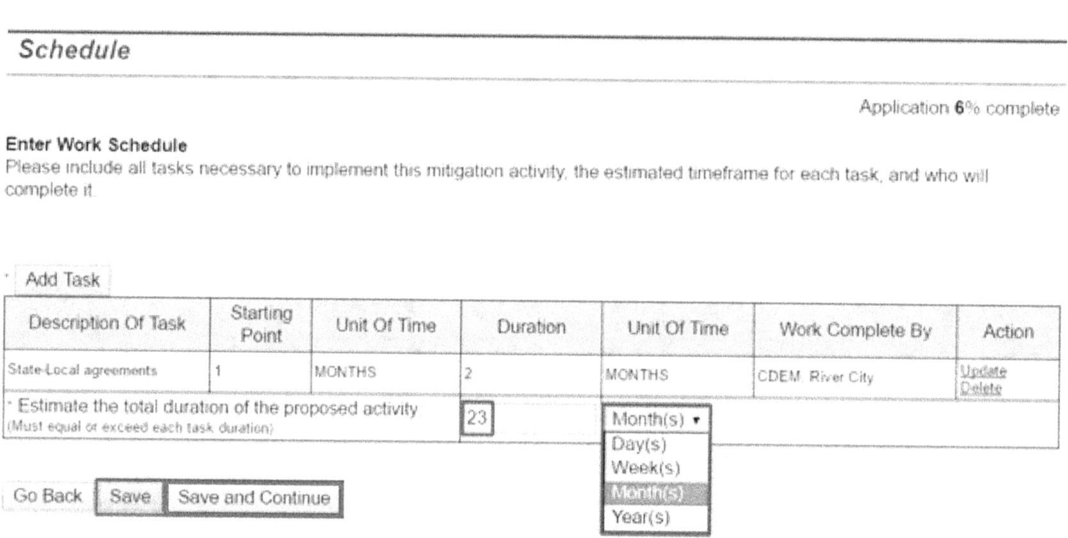

The Schedule screen appears. The screen asks to "Estimate the total duration of the proposed activity." If you total up all the time needed to finish all the tasks for the acquisition and demolition project, it comes to 23 months. So enter "23" in the **Duration** text field and select the "Month(s)" option from the **Unit of Time** drop-down menu. Then, select the **Save** button to add another task. When all tasks are entered, you can select the **Save and Continue** button to move onto the next section of the subapplication.

Cost Estimate Section

The Cost Estimate section provides the detailed line item budget for each proposed activity. If more than one mitigation activity is proposed, then the Cost Estimate is broken out by the activities identified in the Scope of Work section. The cost estimate must be itemized rather than listed as a lump sum. You'll need to have at least two line items for the section to be considered complete. Personnel and Equipment are two common line item costs listed.

You must click the Add Item button to add each new cost item.

Information required for each cost item includes:

- Item Name (i.e., general description of the cost)
- Subgrant Budget Class (selected from a drop-down list)
- Unit Quantity (e.g., 1 ,2 ,3 ,...n)
- Unit Measure (e.g., each, acres, cubic feet, etc.)
- Unit Cost per item
- Cost Estimate

The total of all cost items will be the total Cost Estimate for the subaward.

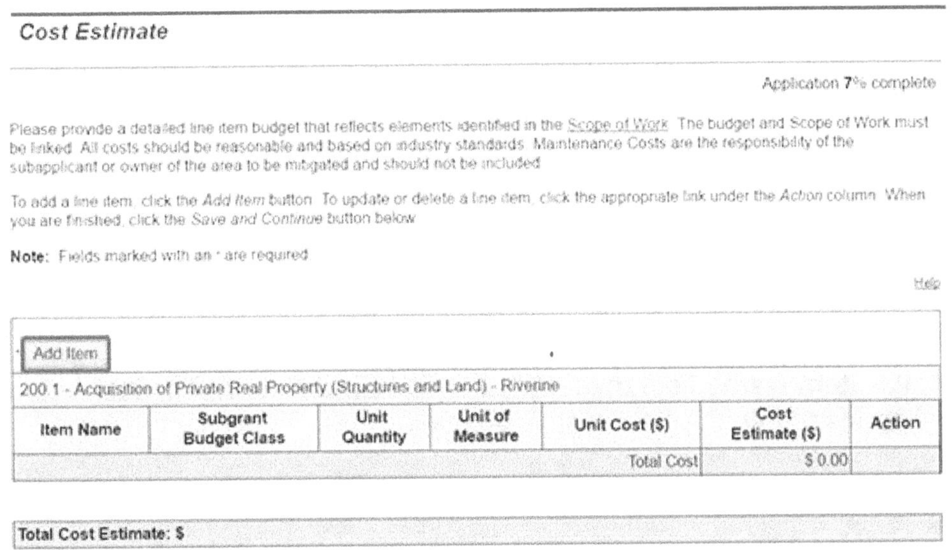

Select this link for a full description of the image.

Complete the Cost Estimate Section

Sally will help you complete the Cost Estimate section for the subapplication. Scroll down to see slideshow captions.

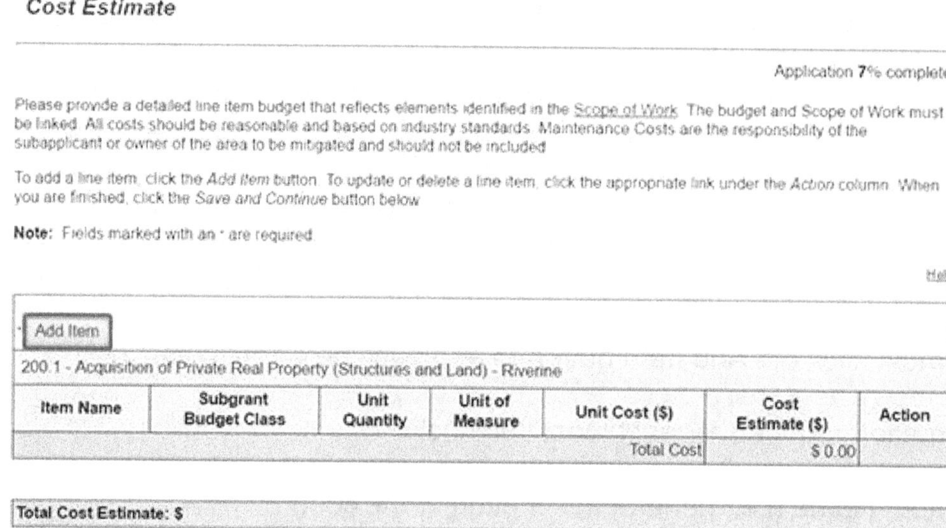

After selecting the Cost Estimate link from the sidebar menu, select the **Add Item** button to add a line item to the River City floodplain acquisition project budget. The budget must be itemized and can't be listed as a single, lump sum.

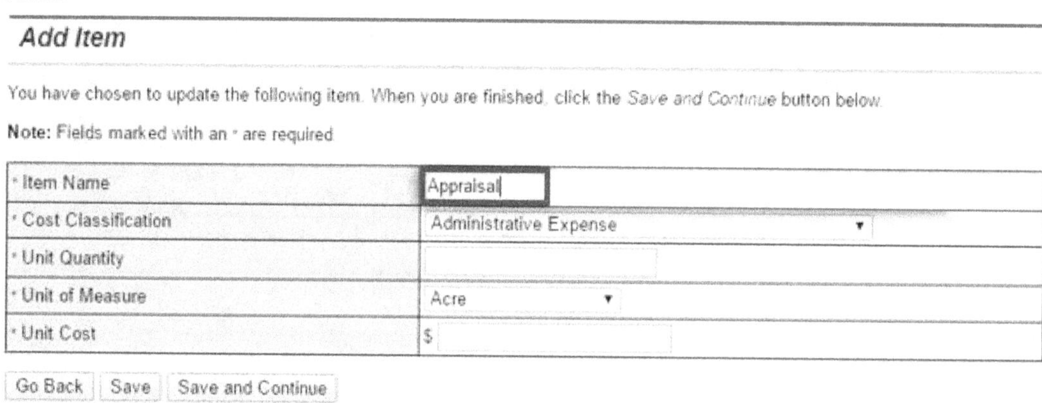

Select the **Item Name** field to identify the first budget item. For our first item, type "Appraisal" into the Item Name text field.

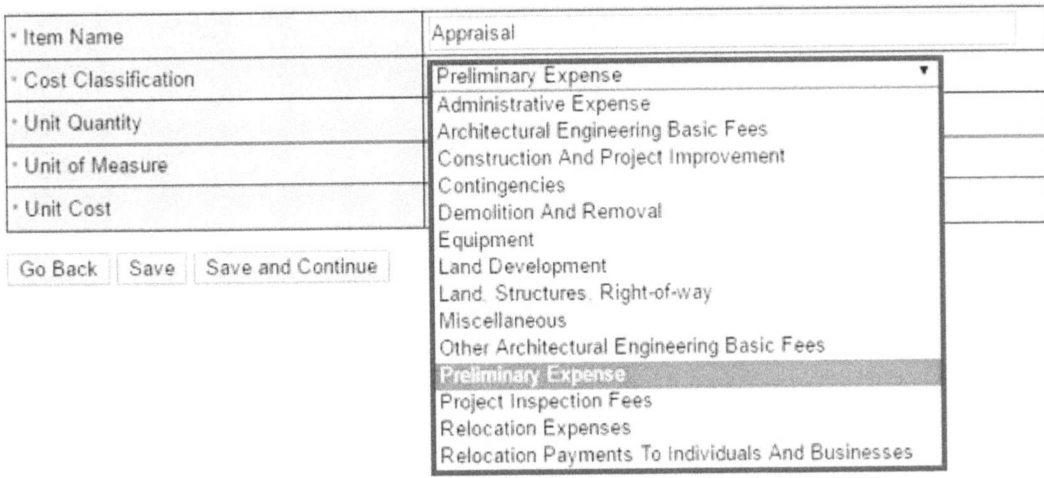

Next, select the **Cost Classification** drop-down menu. This menu has 14 options. Select "Preliminary Expense" for the appraisal budget item.

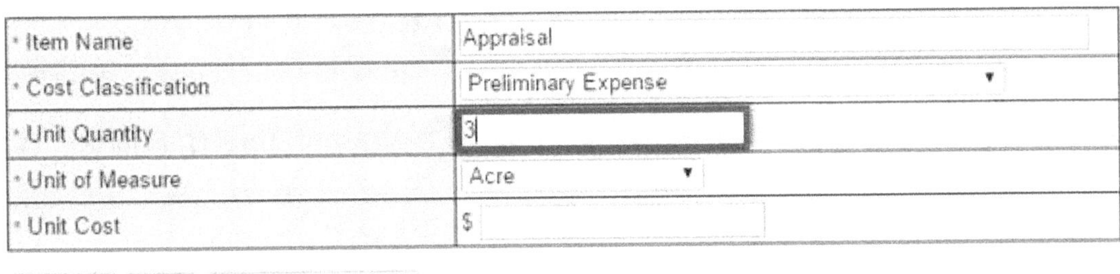

Now you need to select the **Unit Quantity** field. This is where you indicate the number of items that need to be purchased. Since there are three structures that will need to be appraised as a part of the floodplain acquisition project, enter in the number "3."

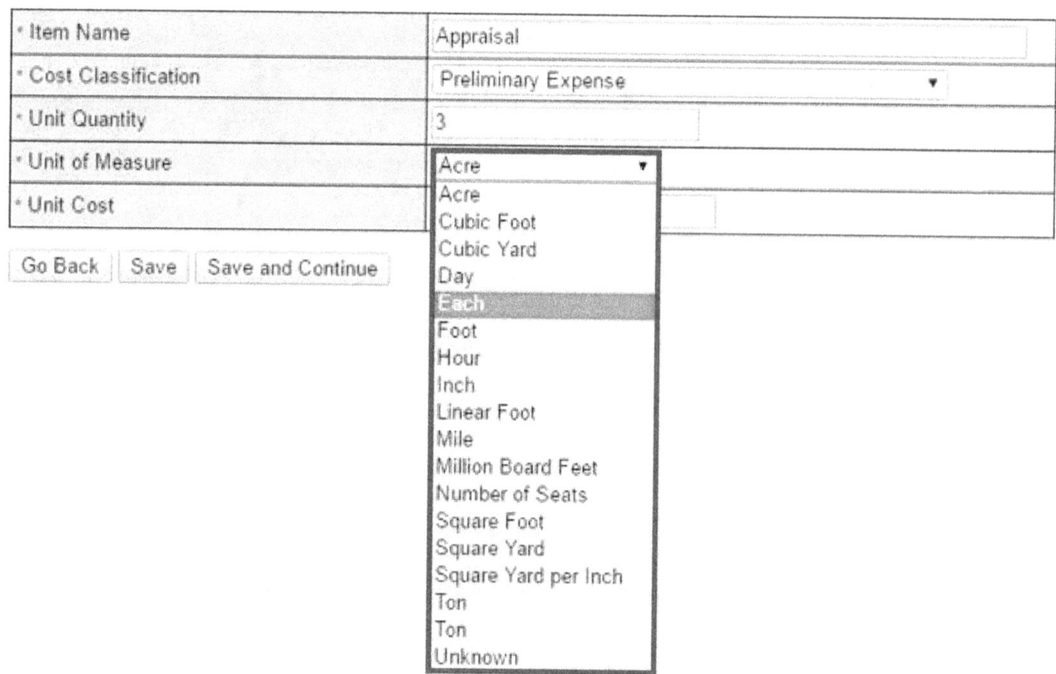

Select the **Unit of Measure** drop-down menu. This menu has 18 options. We want to select the "Each" option.

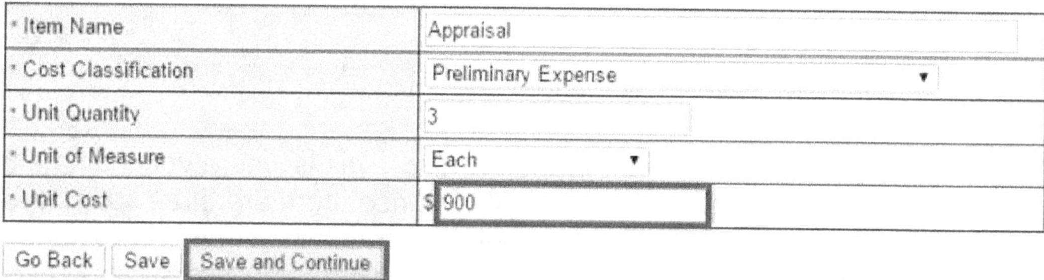

Then, select the **Unit Cost** field. This is where you input the dollar amount for one unit of the item identified. Each appraisal is going to cost $900. So, enter "900" in the text field. Then, select the **Save and Continue** button.

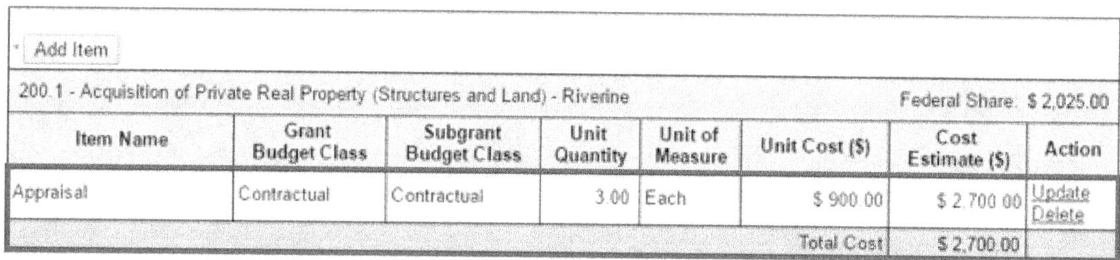

Item Name	Grant Budget Class	Subgrant Budget Class	Unit Quantity	Unit of Measure	Unit Cost ($)	Cost Estimate ($)	Action
Appraisal	Contractual	Contractual	3.00	Each	$ 900.00	$ 2,700.00	Update Delete
					Total Cost	$ 2,700.00	

200.1 - Acquisition of Private Real Property (Structures and Land) - Riverine — Federal Share: $ 2,025.00

Add Item

Total Cost Estimate: $ 2,700.00

Go Back   Save and Continue

You can see that the appraisal line item has been added to the Cost Estimate section. eGrants automatically calculated the amount of the Cost Estimate for the Appraisal item by multiplying the Unit Quantity by the Unit Cost. The Cost Estimate section requires a minimum of two (2) line items. The floodplain acquisition project will have more than that. You'll need to repeat these steps to add the other items.

Cost Share Section

The Cost Share section allows the Subapplicant to identify the total amount and sources of the Non-Federal Cost Share for the subaward. For example, the PDM grant program allows a maximum of 75% of the total cost estimate to be met by federal funds, and so a minimum of 25% of the total cost estimate must be met by non-federal funds. You can adjust the Proposed Non-Federal Share dollar amount to reflect the actual non-federal contribution to the subaward.

Sally will show you how to work on the Cost Share section of the River City subapplication.

Scroll down to see slideshow captions

Cost Share

The Cost Share is automatically calculated to 75% Federal / 25% non-Federal. If you modify the Non-Federal Share amount, click the Recalculate Share button to compute the new Federal and Non-Federal Share Percentages

Please provide the following information. When you are finished, click the Save and Continue button below. Please add the funding source records whose total amount should be greater than or equal to the proposed non-Federal share amount

Note: Fields marked with an * are required

Activity Cost Estimate (If you modify the Federal Share Percentage or Non-Federal Share amount, click the Recalculate Share button to compute the new Federal Share.)	$ 603,480.00	
Federal Share Percentage	75%	Help
Non-Federal Share Percentage	25%	Help
	Dollars	Percentage
* Proposed Federal Share (Calculated based on the Federal Share Percentage) Notes: for L-PDM grants, Federal Share may be up to 90% for small, impoverished community. For SRL, Federal share may be up to 90% when the Applicant has an approved State Mitigation Plan that specifies how it intends to reduce the number of SRL properties.	$	75%
*Proposed Non-Federal Share (Calculated based on the Non-Federal Share Percentage)	$ 150,870.00	25% Recalculate Share

The Cost Share screen displays the funding sources and dollar amounts. The Proposed Non-Federal Share is the amount of money that will come from local government and community funds. The cash and in-kind contributions that River City has earmarked for the floodplain acquisition project total $150,870, so enter that amount in the **Proposed Non-Federal Share** text field. Then, select the **Recalculate Share** button to determine the percentage of the total cost estimate that is represented by the revised non-federal share contributions.

Activity Cost Estimate (If you modify the Federal Share Percentage or Non-Federal Share amount, click the Recalculate Share button to compute the new Federal Share.)	$ 603,480.00	
Federal Share Percentage	75%	Help
Non-Federal Share Percentage	25%	Help
	Dollars	Percentage
* Proposed Federal Share (Calculated based on the Federal Share Percentage) Notes: for L-PDM grants, Federal Share may be up to 90% for small, impoverished community. For SRL, Federal share may be up to 90% when the Applicant has an approved State Mitigation Plan that specifies how it intends to reduce the number of SRL properties.	$ 452,610.00	75%
*Proposed Non-Federal Share (Calculated based on the Non-Federal Share Percentage)	$ 150,870.00	25% Recalculate Share

The **recalculated dollar amounts and percentages** for both the Proposed Federal Share and Proposed Non-Federal Share are displayed.

Cost Share (continued)

The Cost Share section also allows the Subapplicant to identify all of the sources of the non-federal funds and whether each source will be cash or in-kind services. You may list the funding sources by selecting the Add Cost Share button.

Information required for each cost share includes:

- Source agency (e.g., state, local, private non-profit, tribal, etc.)
- Name of source agency
- Funding type (cash or in-kind)
- Amount

This section also has an Attach File button to use to attach a funds commitment letter.

Note   If cost share funds are added, then the total amount of cost share funds must equal the proposed non-federal share dollars in order for the Cost Share section to be complete.

Complete the Cost Share Section

Sally will show you how to complete the Cost Share section for River City Floodplain Acquisition—Phase 1 subapplication.
Scroll down to see slideshow captions.

| Add Cost Share | | | | |
Source Agency	Name of Source Agency	Funding Type	Amount ($)	Action
			Grand Total	$ 0.00	

If you would like to make any comments, please enter them below.

(Maximum 4000 characters)

To attach documents, click the *Attach File* button below.

Attach File
(You will be able to add attachments, once this form is saved.)

To complete the rest of the Cost Share section, select the **Add Cost Share** button.

Add Cost Share

Please provide the following information. When you are finished, click the *Save and Continue* button below.

Note: Fields marked with an * are required.

* Funding Source	Local Agency Funding ▼
	Local Agency Funding
	Other Agency Funding
	Private Non Profit Funding
	State Agency Funding
If other, please specify	
* Name of Funding Source	
* Funding Type	

Then select the **Funding Source** drop-down menu. This menu has four options. Select the "Local Agency Funding" option to provide details about the funds promised by the River City community.

* Funding Source	Local Agency Funding ▼
If other, please specify	
* Name of Funding Source	Office of the Mayor
* Funding Type	Administration ▼
If other, please specify	

Select the **Name of Funding Source** field and type the name of the source. The bulk of the funds will come from the River City government. So, type "Office of the Mayor" in the Name of Funding Source field.

* Funding Source	Local Agency Funding ▼
If other, please specify	
* Name of Funding Source	Office of the Mayor
* Funding Type	Cash ▼
If other, please specify	Administration **Cash** Consulting Fees Engineering Fees Equipment Op/Rental (MM-DD-YYYY e.g. 02-05-2002) Labor Other (MM-DD-YYYY e.g. 02-05-2002) Program Income Supplies
* Amount	
Date of availability	
Funds commitment letter date	

Select the **Funding Type** drop-down menu. This menu has nine options. Select "Cash." The total promised by the River City government also includes an in-kind donation of labor. You will add that cost share later.

* Funding Source	Local Agency Funding ▼
If other, please specify	
* Name of Funding Source	Office of the Mayor
* Funding Type	Cash ▼
If other, please specify	
* Amount	$ 130,870
Date of availability	(MM-DD-YYYY e.g. 02-05-2002)
Funds commitment letter date	(MM-DD-YYYY e.g. 02-05-2002)

Select the **Amount** field. River City will contribute $130,870 to the floodplain acquisition project. So type "130,870" in the Amount field.

* Funding Source	Local Agency Funding ▼
If other, please specify	
* Name of Funding Source	Office of the Mayor
* Funding Type	Cash ▼
If other, please specify	
* Amount	$ 130,870
Date of availability	08-20-2017 (MM-DD-YYYY e.g. 02-05-2002)
Funds commitment letter date	(MM-DD-YYYY e.g. 02-05-2002)

Select the **Date of availability** field. The funds will be released in August 2017. So type "08-20-2017" into the Date of availability field.

· Funding Source	Local Agency Funding ▼
If other, please specify	
· Name of Funding Source	Office of the Mayor
· Funding Type	Cash ▼
If other, please specify	
· Amount	$ 130,870
Date of availability	08-20-2017 (MM-DD-YYYY e.g. 02-05-2002)
Funds commitment letter date	05-12-2017 (MM-DD-YYYY e.g. 02-05-2002)
Attach funds commitment letter	To attach documents, click the *Attach File* button below. Attach File (You will be able to add attachments, once this form is saved.)

Go Back Save **Save and Continue**

Next, select the **Funds commitment letter date** field. The letter from the Mayor's office detailing the budgeted funds is dated May 12, 2017. So enter "05-12-2017" into the Funds commitment letter date field. Then, select the **Save** button.

· Funding Type	Cash ▼
If other, please specify	
· Amount	$ 130870.00
Date of availability	06-20-2017 (MM-DD-YYYY e.g. 02-05-2002)
Funds commitment letter date	05-20-2017 (MM-DD-YYYY e.g. 02-05-2002)
Attach funds commitment letter	To attach documents, click the *Attach File* button below. Attach File

Go Back Save Save and Continue

Now, select the **Attach File** button. You will follow the steps to attach an electronic file like I showed you earlier.

Attach funds commitment letter	To attach documents, click the *Attach File* button below.		
	Name	Date Attached	Action
	Acquisition_AttachmentR_FundAuthorizationResolution_Draft.docx	06-14-2017	Delete
	Attach File		

Go Back Save **Save and Continue**

The file name now appears on the Cost Share screen. Select the **Save and Continue** button.

Non-Federal Funds

Please add your non-Federal funds below by clicking the *Add Cost Share* button. To update or delete funds click the appropriate link under the *Action* column.

Add Cost Share

Source Agency	Name of Source Agency	Funding Type	Amount ($)	Action
Local Agency Funding	Office of the Mayor	Cash	$ 130,870.00	View Details Update Delete
		Grand Total	$ 130,870.00	

You can see that the Cost Share you added is now listed on the Cost Share screen.

Cost Effectiveness Section

The Cost Effectiveness section collects information about the cost effectiveness of the proposed mitigation activity. The information to be provided here is based on a FEMA-approved Benefit-Cost Analysis (BCA). The Benefit-Cost Ratio (BCR) is calculated by dividing the Net Present Value of the Project Benefits by the Total Projected Cost Estimate for the project. Select the Attach button to upload Benefit-Cost Analysis documentation.

Maintenance costs are included in the BCA, so it is important to use the Total Project Costs figures generated through that analysis when completing this section.

This section is not required for planning subapplications.

Cost Effectiveness

Application 21% complete

Please provide the following information. Cost Effectiveness is based on the **entire project**. When complete, click the *Save and Continue* button below to continue to the next section.

Note: All Projects require Cost Effectiveness data. Please see the Benefit Cost web page for more information.

Attach the Benefit Cost Analysis (BCA), if completed for this project.

Name	Date Attached	Action

Attach

Net Present Value of Project Benefits (A)	$ 1176786
Total Project Cost Estimate (B) (Note: The Total Project Cost from the Benefit Cost Analysis (BCA) should be entered here vs the total from the Cost Estimate section of this application, as maintenance costs are not eligible for grant funding but are considered in the BCA.)	$ 603480
What is the Benefit Cost Ratio for the entire project (A/B)?	

Select this link for the full text of the image.

Environmental/Historic Preservation Review Section

The Environmental/Historic Preservation Review section is required for project subapplications only. The EHP Review section does not appear on planning, management costs, or technical assistance subapplications.

The EHP Review section is broken down into 11 parts covering relevant environmental laws and executive orders. Responses to each of these sections allow FEMA Reviewers to identify any potential environmental impacts that may result from the mitigation activity and to identify remedies to eliminate or lessen any adverse impact.

To complete this section, you can either move through Sections A–K sequentially using the Save and Continue button, or use the drop-down menu to navigate to any of the sections.

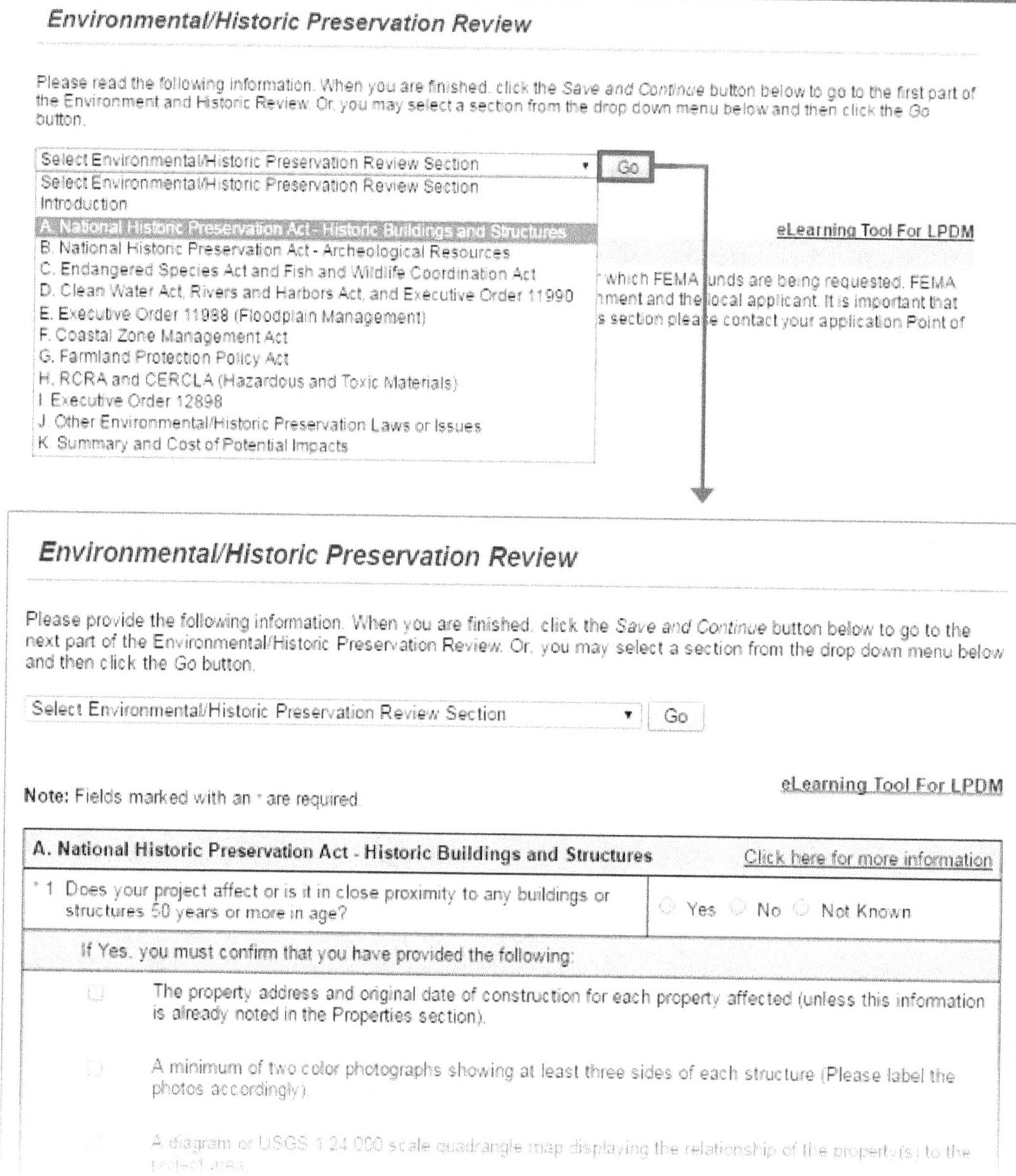

<u>Select this link for the full text of the image.</u>

Evaluation Section

The Evaluation section is used for entering detailed information on the Subapplicant and the proposed project or planning activities for use by the Applicant during the review process, and for PDM subapplications, during the National Review Process.

Specific details that need to be collected include:

- Community participation in programs such as the Community Rating System and Firewise Communities
- Community's adoption of building codes
- Desired outcomes, methodologies, performance expectations, timelines, milestones, and staff and resource plans
- Partners' involvement, long-term financial and social benefits, and outreach activities
- Percentage of population benefitting, as well as the cost-effectiveness (BCA) of projects

Note The Evaluation section is required only for PDM subapplications. If the subapplication is being submitted to the FMA grant program, the Subapplicant may check "Not Applicable."

Evaluation

Please click the link below to complete or modify the different parts of the *Evaluation Information* section. If the section is not applicable, check the *Not Applicable* box provided below. When you are finished, click the *Save and Continue* button.

By checking the Not Applicable box and not providing the information in this section, I understand that this application may not be selected for the Pre-Disaster Mitigation - Competitive Grant Program (PDMC) nor Legislative Pre-Disaster Mitigation Program (LPDM).

Incomplete	☐ Not applicable

Evaluation (Page 1 of 2)

Please provide the following information. When you are finished, click the *Save and Continue* button below.

Note: Fields marked with an * are required.

		Help
* Is the recipient participating in the Community Rating System (CRS)?	○ Yes ○ No	Help
If yes, what is their CRS rating?	▼	
* Is the recipient a Cooperating Technical Partner (CTP)?	○ Yes ○ No	Help
* Is the recipient a Firewise Community?	○ Yes ○ No	Help
If yes, please provide their Firewise Community number.		
* Has the recipient adopted building codes consistent with the International Codes?	○ Yes ○ No	Help
* Has the recipient adopted the National Fire Protection Association (NFPA) 5000 Code?	○ Yes ○ No	Help
* Have the recipient's building codes been assessed on the Building Code Effectiveness Grading Schedule (BCEGS)?	○ Yes ○ No	Help
If yes, what is their BCEGS rating?	▼	
* Is this a small, impoverished community?	○ Yes ○ No	Help

Select this link for the full text of the image.

Assurances and Certifications Section

This section of the subapplication will appear only if Assurances and Certifications is enabled by the Applicant in the administration preferences. The Assurances and Certifications section is intended to provide documents listing federal requirements for FEMA federal awards. There are three documents that may appear in this section. The form contained in Part I differs based on whether or not the proposed activities entail construction.

FEMA Form 20-16A, Assurances Non-Construction Programs: This document asks the Subapplicant to certify that it will comply with a series of requirements including non-discrimination, environmental standards, and audits. If the subapplication circumstances do not include a Non-Construction program, select "Not Applicable" for this form.

or

FEMA Form 20-16B, Assurances Construction Programs: This document asks the Subapplicant to certify that it will comply with a series of requirements including non-discrimination, environmental standards, and audits. If the subapplication circumstances do not include a Construction program, select "Not Applicable" for this form.

FEMA Form 20-16C, Certification Regarding Lobbying; Debarment, Suspension and Other Responsibility Matters; and Drug-Free Workplace Requirements: This document asks the Subapplicant to certify that it will adhere to requirements regarding lobbying, debarment, suspension, and other responsibility matters as well as drug-free workplace requirements.

SF-LLL, Disclosure of Lobbying Activities: This document asks the Subapplicant to disclose its lobbying activities. Complete this only if you are applying for a subaward of more than $100,000 and have lobbying activities using non-federal funds. If those circumstances do not apply, select "Not Applicable" for this form.

Assurances and Certifications

The documents listed below contain the Federal requirements for all FEMA grants including the right of the Federal government to review the grant activity. Please read these documents carefully. The Assurances and Certifications must be read, signed, and electronically submitted as a part of the application.

Please click the link in the status column to view forms.

Forms	Status
Part I Assurances **Construction** Programs.	Incomplete
	☐ Not Applicable
Part II Certifications Regarding Lobbying, Debarment, Suspension and Other Responsibilities Matters, and Drug-Free Workplace Requirements.	Incomplete
Part III SF-LLL, Disclosure of Lobbying Activities (Complete only if applying for a grant of more than $100,000 and have lobbying activities using Non-Federal funds. See the Certifications Regarding Lobbying; Debarment, Suspension and Other Responsibilities Matters; and Drug-Free Workplace Requirements form for lobbying activities definition.)	Incomplete
	☐ Not Applicable

NOTE: By signing the certification regarding debarment, suspension, and other responsibility matters for primary covered transaction, the applicant agrees that, should the proposed covered transaction be entered into, it shall not knowingly enter into any lower tier covered transaction with a person who is debarred, suspended, declared ineligible, or voluntarily excluded from participation in this covered transaction, unless authorized by FEMA entering into this transaction. The applicant further agrees by submitting this application that it will include the clause titled "Certification Regarding Debarment, Suspension, Ineligibility and Voluntary Exclusion-Lower Tier Covered Transaction" provided by the FEMA Regional Office entering into this covered transaction, without modification, in all lower tier covered transactions and in all solicitations for lower tier covered transactions. (Refer to 44 CFR Part 17.)

<u>Select this link for the full text of the image.</u>

Comments and Attachments Section

Many sections of the subapplication form have a Comments text field and an Attachment button. To facilitate the review of the subapplication by the Applicant and FEMA reviewers, it is best to add comments and attachments directly to the section they concern.

- **Comments** are text only and may provide additional information.
- **Attachments** may be any file type up to 50 MB (e.g., Word documents, Excel spreadsheets, PDF files, etc.). For larger files or paper documents, you may indicate to the Applicant that you will be sending additional documentation by mail and provide tracking information. The attachment file name should clearly reflect the contents of the attachment.

This section will appear for all types of subapplications and it consolidates all the comments and attachments in the subapplication for easy review. It also provides the Subapplicant with an opportunity to provide information not covered by the subapplication sections. This may include any information that could potentially help the Applicant or FEMA come to a decision regarding this subapplication or provide documentation to support information provided in the subapplication.

Completing the Comments and Attachments Section

Sally is ready to show you how to complete the Comments and Attachments section for the River City Floodplain Acquisition subapplication.
Scroll down to see slideshow captions.

Comments and Attachments

This section will enable you to add comments or attach files to supplement any section you have already completed. To add a comment or attachment click on the Add button. You may also update or delete any comments. To update or delete a comment, click on the link in the Action column.

Name of Section	Comment	Attachment	Date Attached	Action

Add

Go Back   Save and Continue

We are going to need to attach some supporting documents to the subapplication. While it is best to attach a document directly to the section to which it pertains, you can also do it in the Comments and Attachments section of the subapplication. On the Comments and Attachments screen, select the **Add** button.

Add Comments and Attachments

You may enter your new comments in the box below, or you may include additional information as an attachment. Please be sure to provide the name of the section to which your comment or attachment refers.

Name of section:

Application Level ▼	
Application Level	
Community	...e any comments, please enter them below.
Mitigation Plan	
Scope of Work	
Cost Share	
Cost Effectiveness	
Evaluation	

Select the **Name of Section** drop-down menu to identify to which section of the subapplication you want to attach the document. The menu has seven options. We have a Word document we want to attach to the Scope of Work section, so select the "Scope of Work" option.

Add Comments and Attachments

You may enter your new comments in the box below, or you may include additional information as an attachment. Please be sure to provide the name of the section to which your comment or attachment refers.

Name of section:

Scope of Work ▼

If you would like to make any comments, please enter them below.

(Maximum 4000 characters)

Rationale and Plan for Acquisition Project

To attach documents, click the *Attachments* button below. (You may include Photographs; Property deed; Tax assessment; Tax parcel map; Flood Insurance Rate Map (FIRM) with project site marked; Insurance settlements/documentation; Engineering or design specifications; etc.)

Name	Date Attached	Action

Attachments

Go Back   Save   Save and Continue

You need to provide a short explanation about the document you are attaching. The document we want to attach explains the rationale for the project. So, select the **Comments** field and type "Rationale and Plan for Acquisition Project." Then, select the **Attachments** button. You can either attach the document as an electronic file or send it as a paper document through the mail. I will show you how to provide information for both processes in eGrants.

Electronic Files

Within the Comments and Attachments section, Subapplicants are provided with the opportunity to attach various files that provide additional information to the Applicant. These files may be either paper or electronic files.

Sally will show how you how to attach an electronic file in the Comments and Attachments section of the River City Floodplain Acquisition—Phase 1 subapplication.

Scroll down to see slideshow captions.

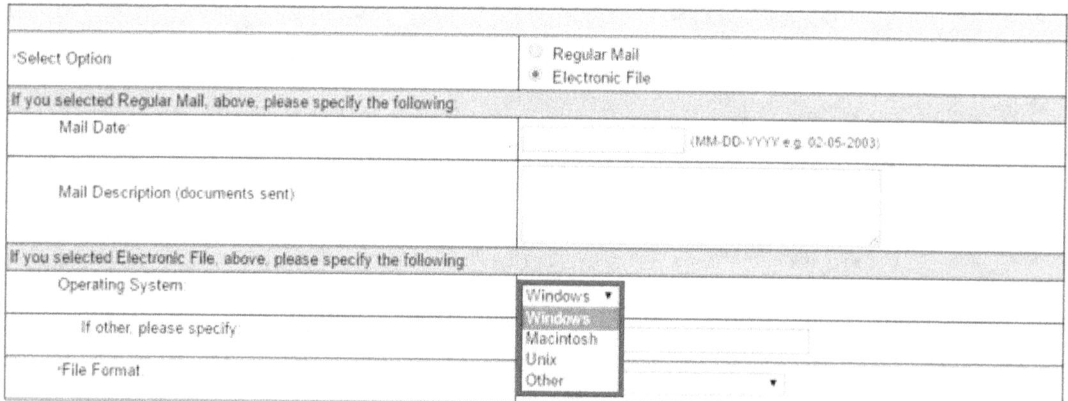

After you have selected the Attach File button, you will see the Attach Document screen appear. You will need to upload the Word document to be able to attach it to the Scope of Work section of the subapplication. Select the **Electronic File** radio button to upload the file to the subapplication.

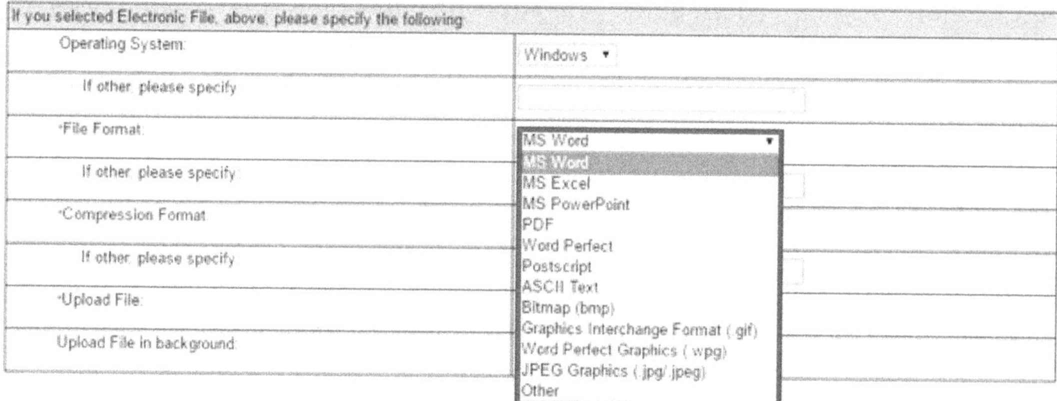

It is necessary to identify the computer operating system that was used to create the file. To do that, select the **Operating System** drop-down menu. This menu has four options: Windows, Macintosh, Unix, and Other. We have Windows ® on this computer, so select the "Windows" option.

We also need to identify the software used to create the file being attached. Select the **File Format** drop-down menu. This menu has 12 options. Since we want to upload a Word document, select the "MS Word" option.

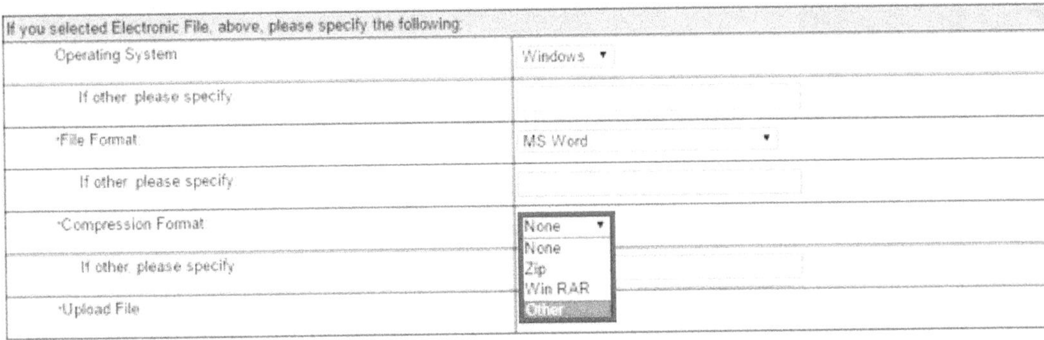

Sometimes large files are compressed (or zipped) to make it easier to upload and download them. You need to indicate if you have compressed the file you wish to upload. Select the **Compression Format** drop-down menu. This menu has four options: None, Zip, Win RAR, and Other. The Word document we want to attach doesn't have a very large file size, so we won't need to compress it in order to upload it. So, select the "None" option.

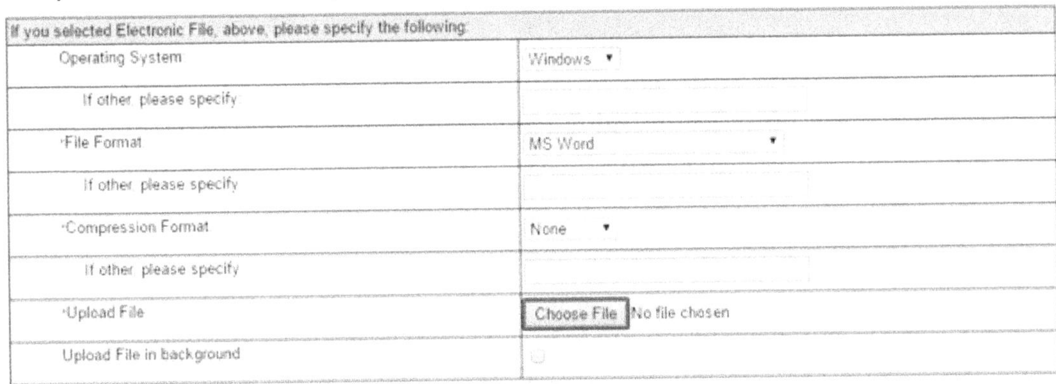

To find the file you want to upload, select the **Choose File** button.

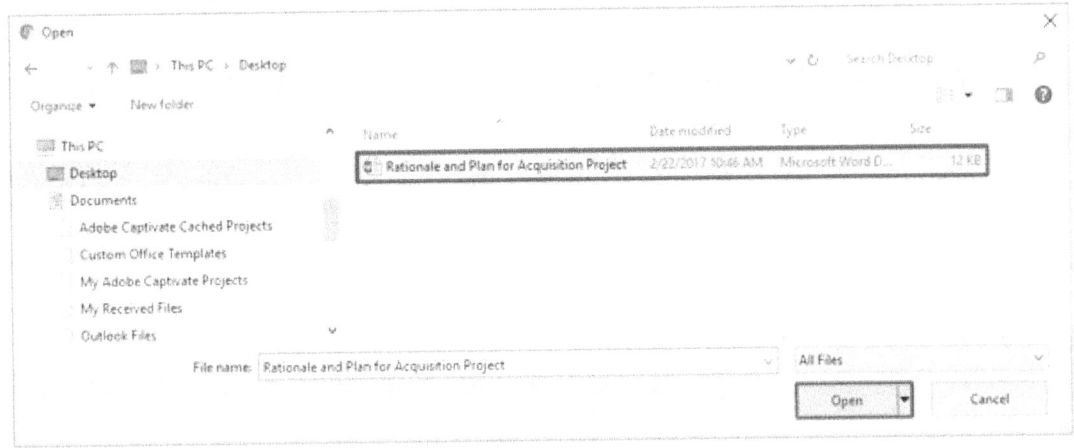

This opens the file navigator on your computer so you can navigate to and select the file you want to attach. Select the document titled "Rationale and Plan for Acquisition Project" and select the **Open** button.

Save and Continue

Then, select the **Save and Continue** button.

If you selected Electronic File, above, please specify the following	
Operating System	Windows ▼
If other, please specify	
*File Format	MS Word ▼
If other, please specify	
*Compression Format	None ▼
If other, please specify	
*Upload File	Choose File Rationale a…roject.docx
Upload File in background	☐

Go Back   Save and Continue

You will see an abbreviated version of the file name appear to the right of the Choose File button. That serves as a confirmation that the document uploaded successfully. Select the **Save and Continue** button to move onto the next section.

Attaching Paper Files

In many cases, Subapplicants find that documents they want to attach within the Comments and Attachments section may exist only as a hard copy, or in a paper form. In that case, they must mail the files directly to the Applicant. However, information about the mailing should be entered into the eGrants system. This ensures that you create a complete subapplication file with reference to any non-electronic information that was mailed. Once received, the Applicant should make every effort to scan those documents to create an electronic file.

Sally wants to show you how to complete the Comments and Attachments section of the River City subapplication to reference a supporting paper document that was sent through the mail.

Scroll down to see slideshow captions

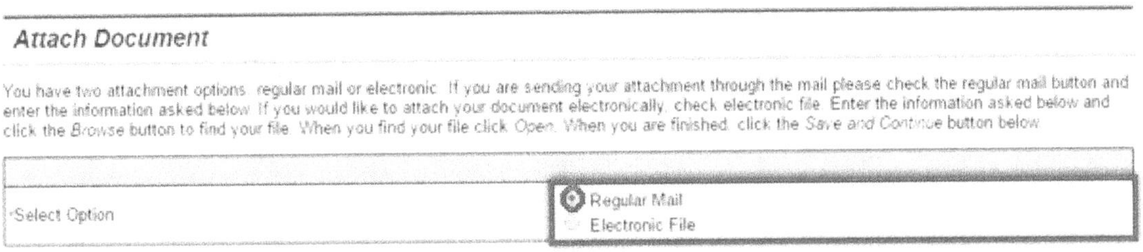

Attach Document

You have two attachment options: regular mail or electronic. If you are sending your attachment through the mail please check the regular mail button and enter the information asked below. If you would like to attach your document electronically, check electronic file. Enter the information asked below and click the *Browse* button to find your file. When you find your file click *Open*. When you are finished, click the *Save and Continue* button below.

Select Option	◉ Regular Mail ○ Electronic File

If the document we want to attach is not available as an electronic file or is too large to upload, we can still include it as supporting evidence in the subapplication. We just need to send it to the Applicant through the mail. To indicate that you are sending a document via the U.S. Postal system, select the **Regular Mail** radio button to the right of the **Select Option** prompt on the Attach Document screen.

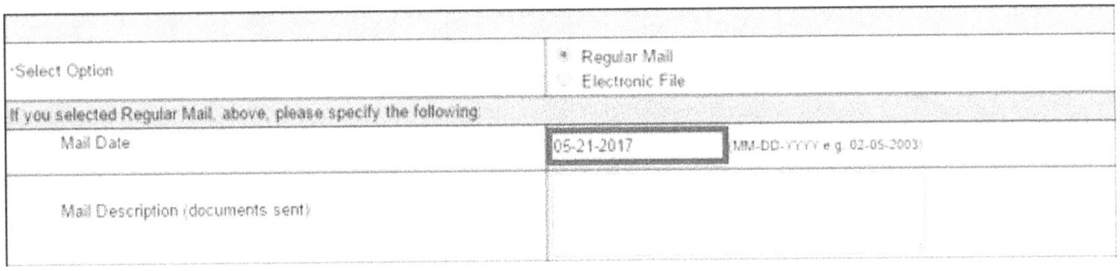

Select Option	⦿ Regular Mail ○ Electronic File
If you selected Regular Mail, above, please specify the following:	
Mail Date	05-21-2017 (MM-DD-YYYY e.g. 02-05-2003)
Mail Description (documents sent)	

To create a record of the transaction, you'll need to enter the date when the document was put into the mail. I mailed the document yesterday. So select the **Mail Date** field and type "05-21-2017" into the text field.

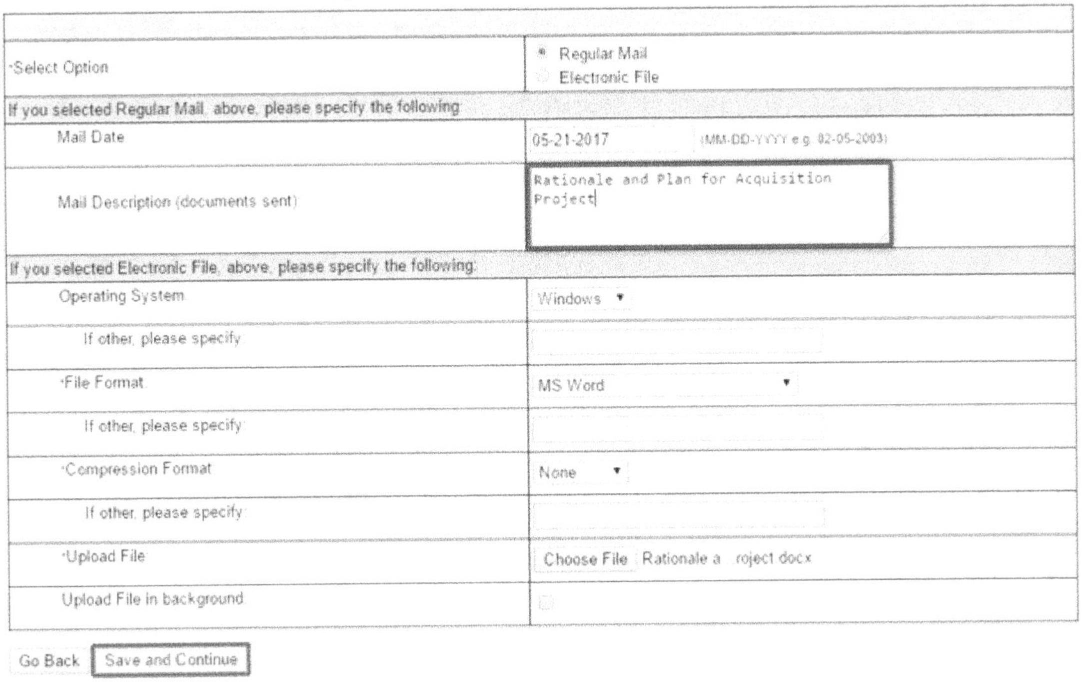

Select Option	⦿ Regular Mail ○ Electronic File
If you selected Regular Mail, above, please specify the following:	
Mail Date	05-21-2017 (MM-DD-YYYY e.g. 02-05-2003)
Mail Description (documents sent)	Rationale and Plan for Acquisition Project
If you selected Electronic File, above, please specify the following:	
Operating System	Windows ▾
If other, please specify	
File Format	MS Word ▾
If other, please specify	
Compression Format	None ▾
If other, please specify	
Upload File	Choose File Rationale a...roject.docx
Upload File in background	☐

Go Back   Save and Continue

Next, select the **Mail Description** field. Like with the electronic file, you need to type a brief description of the item being sent. You can type "Rationale and Plan for Acquisition Project" in the text field. Then, select the **Save and Continue** button.

Document(s) Mailed

Attachment Option	Regular Mail
Mail Details	
Mail Date	05-21-2017
Mail Description	Rationale and Plan for Acquisition Project

Go Back   Edit   Attachments   Save and Continue

The Document(s) Mailed screen appears and displays the mail date and the description of the item being sent via Regular Mail.

Lesson 6 Summary

You have finished the lesson on completing subapplications. In this lesson, you learned that:

- You can search for an un-submitted subapplication.
- You can review your progress toward completing your subapplication from both the **Application Status** and **Review and Submit** sections.
- Information regarding the Subapplicant, the community impacted, and affected properties are captured in the **Subapplicant, Contact Information, Community,** and **Properties** sections. Planning, management costs, and technical assistance Subapplicants do **not** need to complete the Properties section.
- The hazard mitigation activities that are planned, the proposed schedule, details about the estimated costs, funding sources, and the analysis of the benefit of the activities vs. the cost are documented in the **Mitigation Activity Information, Scope of Work, Schedule, Cost Estimate, Cost Share,** and **Cost Effectiveness** sections. Planning, management costs, and technical assistance Subapplicants do not need to complete the Cost Effectiveness section.
- Agreements to adhere to a variety of federal employment, environmental, historic preservation, and other laws and FEMA regulations are documented in the **Environmental/Historical Preservation Review** and **Assurances and Certifications** sections. An Applicant may or may not require a Subapplicant to complete the Assurances and Certifications section.
- If applying to the PDM grant program, Subapplicants must complete the **Evaluation** section so their subapplication can be assigned a priority status.
- Many of the subapplication sections include a Comments text field and an Attachments button for uploading electronic document files. However, Subapplicants can add additional information to their subapplication using the **Comments and Attachments** section. Subapplicants can also indicate that they are sending additional documentation to the Applicant by mail.

Lesson 7

Acquisition Scenario

Name: Sally Watkins

Problem: Sally works as City Manager in River City. Her current task is to assist the Mayor in finding funding for a large project. The project involves the purchase and demolition of three properties along the Washburn River. In past years, these properties have been repeatedly flooded. The Mayor wishes to ensure that these properties will not be flooded again and wants to reduce the impacts to families living in his community by seeking financial assistance to acquire the properties.

To date: Sally has shown you how to create a subapplication in eGrants and you have completed the majority of its sections.

Listen to Sally
Audio transcript

Your Next Step: You will need to ask Sally's co-worker to check over the subapplication to ensure that you have entered everything correctly.

Hi. It's Sally Watkins here. Thank you for working so hard on your first subapplication for River City. I know you have filled out most of the subapplication, but I'd like you to have my co-worker, Michael, go through and check to make sure that you've done it correctly before we submit it. You will need to give him access to the subapplication.

Why Provide Access?

Within eGrants, a user has the ability to grant, update, or revoke access to their subapplication. Some of the reasons to grant someone else access to a subapplication include the following situations:

- **Vacation:** Arturo is creating a subapplication, but he is about to leave for a two-week vacation. He doesn't want work on the subapplication to stop while he's gone. He gives Teresa, a co-worker, access to the subapplication so she can continue entering data in his absence.
- **Advice:** Sayid, a new employee, has completed his first subapplication, but he isn't sure that everything was entered correctly. He gives Claire, a more experienced eGrants user, access to his subapplication so that

she can check his work and make sure that information has been entered correctly.

- **Sharing:** LaTonya, Destiny, and James are all involved with a proposed project to reduce recurring damage due to coastal erosion. They are completing a subapplication in the hopes of receiving funds for their proposed project. LaTonya creates the subapplication and provides access to Destiny and James so that they may help enter the information on the proposed project.

Levels of Access

When providing someone access to a subapplication, different levels of access can be provided and more than one level may be provided.

- **Sign/Submit:** This is the highest level of access, and it allows a Subapplicant to review, sign, and submit a subapplication.
- **Create/Edit:** This is the middle level of access, and it allows an eGrants user to view, create, and update a subapplication, but not to sign or submit it.
- **View/Print:** This is the lowest level of access, and it allows an eGrants user only to view subapplication data and print the information.

Business Rule

There are a few business rules related to the provision of access in eGrants. The first rule states that a subapplication or application owner may authorize or revoke access to the subapplication or application by other eGrants users who are within the same organization. However, the additional user's authorized role will determine the highest level of access he or she may be granted to any subapplication or application. In addition, Subapplicants can share their subapplications with Applicants prior to submitting them to the Applicant.

Example: Tameka, a community official in Alexandria, VA, has Sign/Submit level access in eGrants. She wants to provide Grace with access to her subapplication. However, Grace only has a Create/Edit level of access in eGrants. Therefore, Tameka may not provide Grace with Sign/Submit access to her subapplication, but she may provide Grace with Create/Edit access.

Example: Katie, a state official in Boston, MA, has Create/Edit level access in eGrants. She wants to provide Luong with access to her application. She has completed the application, and it is ready to be reviewed and submitted. Luong has a Sign/Submit level of access in eGrants. Therefore, Katie may provide Luong with Sign/Submit access to her application.

Authorizing Access

eGrants users can authorize access to their subapplications to other registered users in the eGrants system within their same organization. Sally wishes to grant Michael Johnson, her co-worker, access to the River City Floodplain Acquisition—Phase 1 subapplication so that he can verify that you have completed the sections correctly.

To find the access options from the Subgrant Applicant Homepage, select the **Update/Complete an Un-submitted Application(s)** link.

Sally is going to show you how to search for Michael in the eGrants system in order to give him access to the River City Floodplain Acquisition—Phase 1 subapplication.

Scroll down to see slideshow captions.

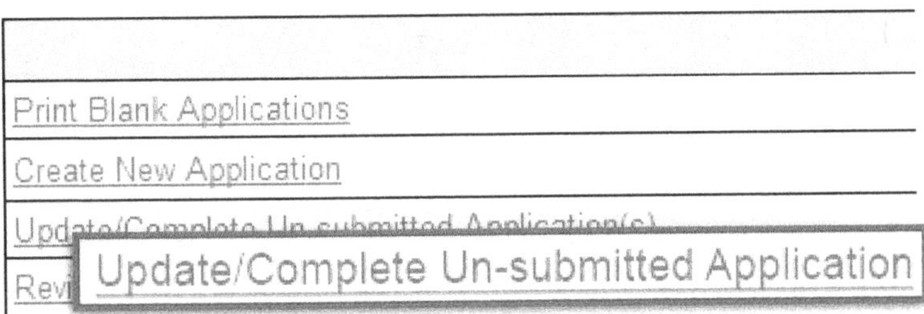

To authorize Michael Johnson's access to the River City Floodplain Acquisition—Phase 1 subapplication, we need to first locate him in the eGrants system. To do that, start on the Subgrant Applicant Homepage and select the **Update/Complete Un-submitted Application(s)** link.

Subgrant Status: Un-submitted Application(s)

Applications that you have started and have not submitted are listed below. To continue work on an application, please select an action for the corresponding application in the table below. To authorize or revoke access to an application, click on the *View Details* link under the *Authorize/Revoke Access* column.

Displaying 1-5 of 1152

Show 5 ▾ Go   Search

Select	Application Year	Application Title	Grant Type	Authorize/Revoke Access	Action
☐	2017	River City Floodplain Acquisition -- Phase 1	Project Application	View Details	Update Application

The Subgrant Status: Un-submitted Application(s) screen appears. You need to select the subapplication you want to provide Michael access to. So locate the River City Floodplain Acquisition—Phase 1 subapplication on the list and select the **View Details** link in the Authorize/Revoke Access column to the right of that title.

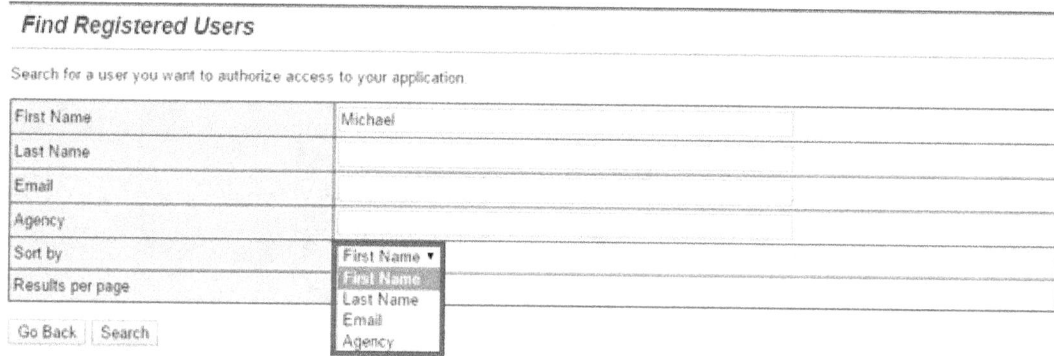

The Find Registered Users screen appears. You will need to search for Michael Johnson's name. You can choose one or more criteria to search for him, including First Name, Last Name, Email address, or Agency. We will search by **First Name.** So type "Michael" in the text field. Since we only need to complete one field to perform a search, we can leave the others blank.

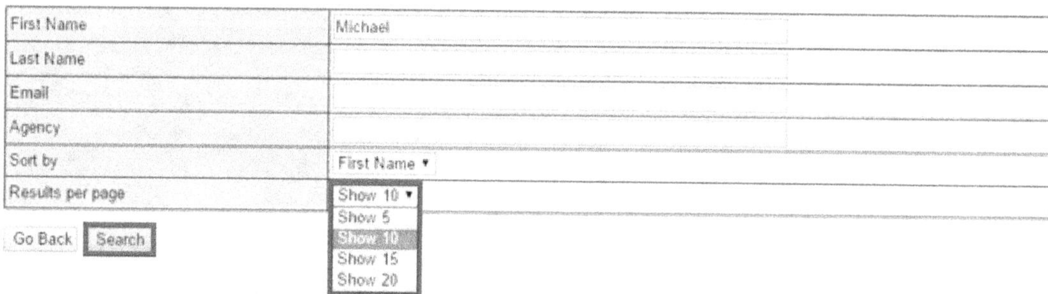

Now, select the **Sort by** drop-down menu. You can see this menu has four options—First Name, Last Name, Email, and Agency. This lets you choose the way in which the results will be sorted. Choose "First Name."

To choose how many results are displayed on a page, select the **Results per page** drop-down menu. This menu has four options. There are likely a few Michaels in the system, so let's select "Show 10." Then select the **Search** button.

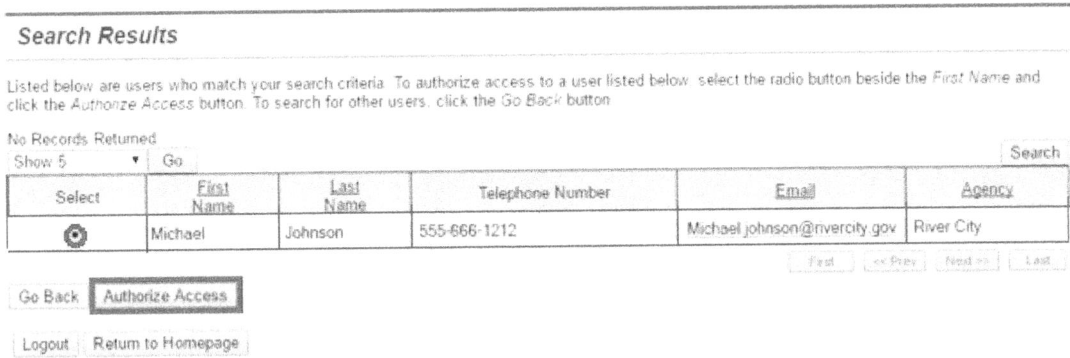

The names matching the search criteria are displayed. To authorize access to our subapplication, select the radio button in the **Select** column to the left of Michael Johnson's name. Then select the **Authorize Access** button. There are some more steps in the Access Authorization process that I need to show you.

Access Level and Duration

When you provide an eGrants user access to your subapplication, you must state which level(s) of access you are authorizing and how long the user will have access to the subapplication. However, you can set the access time limit for as long as you wish.

Sally wants you to provide Michael Johnson with Create/Edit access to the River City Floodplain Acquisition—Phase 1 subapplication. However, she believes Michael only needs a short period of time to review the subapplication.

Scroll down to see slideshow captions.

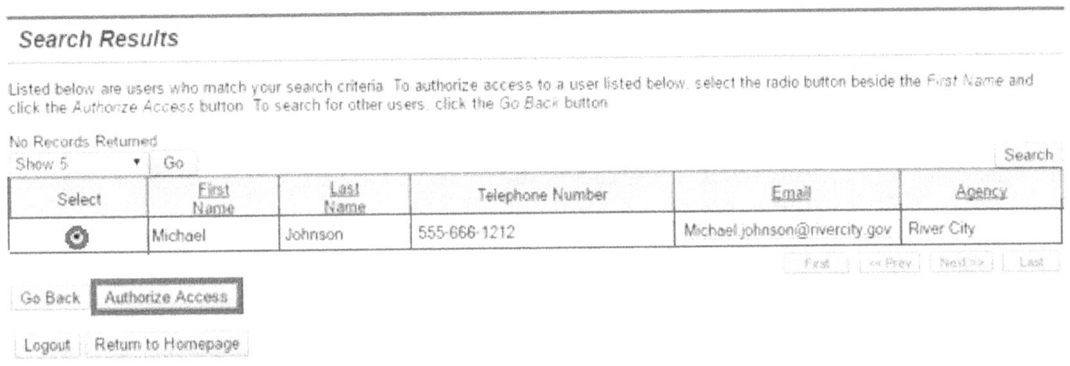

Let's continue the Access Authorization process. We found Michael's name on the Registered User list. Now we need to authorize his access to the River City Floodplain Acquisition—Phase 1 subapplication. Select the radio button in the **Select** column to the left of his name. Then, select the **Authorize Access** button.

User Information	
Title	Public Works Manager
Username	mmjohnson2
First Name	Michael
Middle Initial	
Last Name	Johnson
Telephone	555-666-1212
Email	Michael.johnson@rivercity.gov
Access Information	
·Permissions	☑ View/Print ☑ Create/Edit ☐ Sign/Submit (Permissions can be View only, View & Create, View & Sign or All)
·Period of Time	20 (e.g. 30)
·Unit of Time	Day(s) ▼ (e.g. Days)

Now, scroll down to the bottom of the Update Access screen. To provide Michael with Create/Edit access, you also need to provide him with the lower level of View/Print access. Select the **View/Print** and **Create/Edit** checkboxes.

Access Information	
·Permissions	☑ View/Print ☑ Create/Edit ☐ Sign/Submit (Permissions can be View only, View & Create, View & Sign or All)
·Period of Time	20 (e.g. 30)
·Unit of Time	Day(s) ▼ (e.g. Days) Day(s) Week(s) Month(s) Year(s)

Now, we need to identify how long we want him to have access to the subapplication. I think he might need about three weeks to be able to review it. Let's say 20 days. So, type "20" in the **Period of Time** text field. Select the **Unit of Time** drop-down menu. This menu has four options. Select the "Day(s)" option.

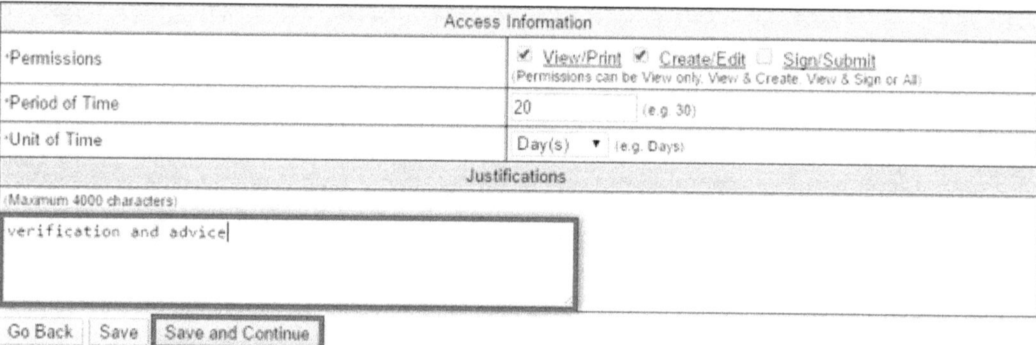

Access Information		
·Permissions	☑ View/Print ☑ Create/Edit ☐ Sign/Submit (Permissions can be View only, View & Create, View & Sign or All)	
·Period of Time	20 (e.g. 30)	
·Unit of Time	Day(s) ▼ (e.g. Days)	
Justifications		
(Maximum 4000 characters)		
verification and advice		

Go Back | Save | Save and Continue

When you provide an eGrants user access to your application, you need to explain why the access is necessary. Select the **justifications** field. This is where you need to type a short explanation. Type "verification and advice." Then, select the **Save and Continue** button.

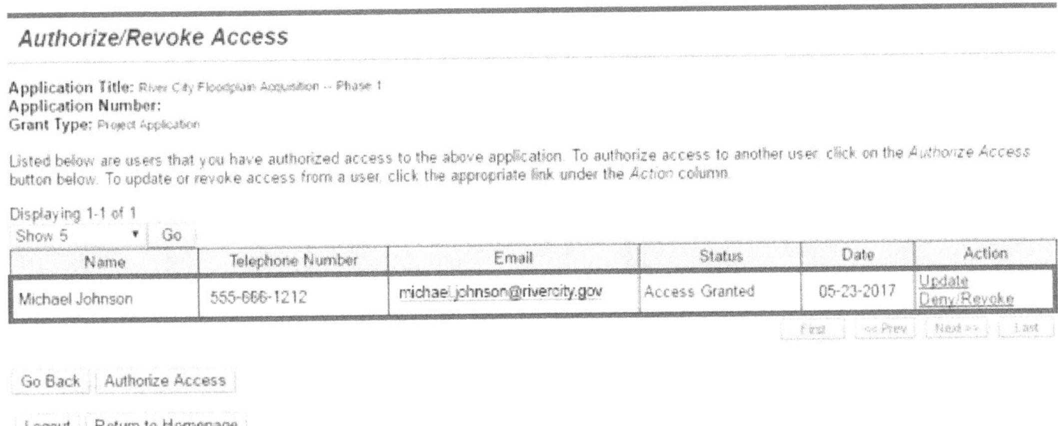

Authorize/Revoke Access

Application Title: River City Floodplain Acquisition -- Phase 1
Application Number:
Grant Type: Project Application

Listed below are users that you have authorized access to the above application. To authorize access to another user, click on the *Authorize Access* button below. To update or revoke access from a user, click the appropriate link under the *Action* column.

Displaying 1-1 of 1
Show 5   ▾   Go

Name	Telephone Number	Email	Status	Date	Action
Michael Johnson	555-666-1212	michael.johnson@rivercity.gov	Access Granted	05-23-2017	Update Deny/Revoke

First   << Prev   Next >>   Last

Go Back   Authorize Access

Logout   Return to Homepage

Now, we can see Michael's name on the Authorize/Revoke Access screen. From this screen, you could change the access privileges of another user or return to the Subgrant Applicant Homepage.

Updating Access

There are a variety of reasons that you may need to update or change the level or duration of access you've provided to an eGrants user.

You learn that Michael Johnson has just been promoted, and his new position has signature authority for River City. Sally wants to update Michael's access privileges to the Sign/Submit level so he can submit the completed River City Floodplain Acquisition subapplication to the Applicant.

Scroll down to see slideshow captions.

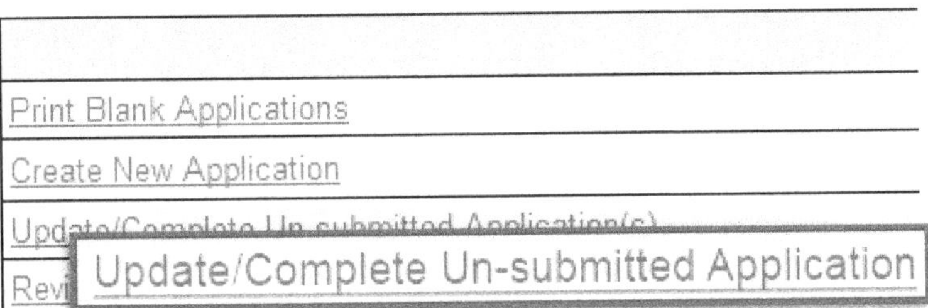

Looking ahead to when the River City Floodplain Acquisition application is complete, I would like Michael to sign and submit it on behalf of River City. We will need to update his access level so he can do that. Go to the Subgrant Applicant Homepage, and select the **Update/Complete Un-submitted Application(s)** link.

Select	Application Year	Application Title	Grant Type	Authorize/Revoke Access	Action
☐	2017	River City Floodplain Acquisition -- Phase 1	Project Application	View Details	Update Application

On the Subgrant Status: Un-submitted Applications(s) screen you need to find the River City Floodplain Acquisition—Phase 1 subapplication so we can modify Michael's access privileges to it. Now, select the **View Details** link in the Authorize/Revoke Access column to the right of the subapplication title

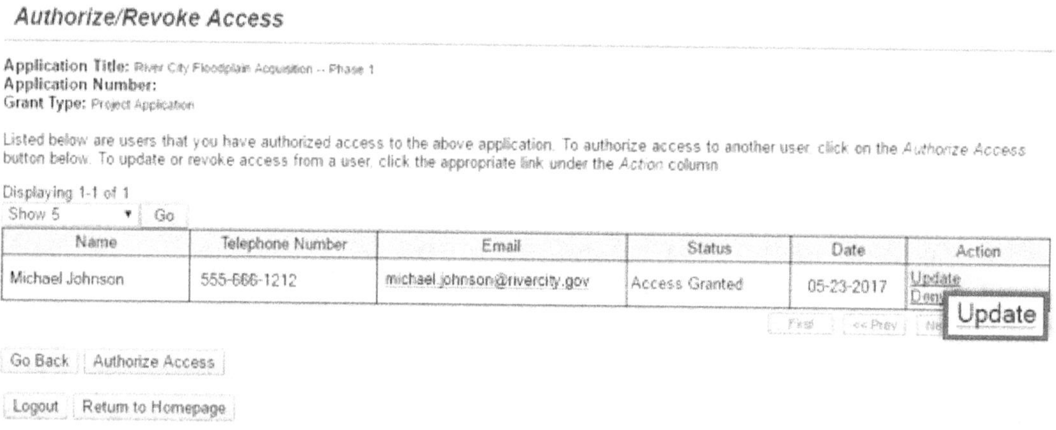

Name	Telephone Number	Email	Status	Date	Action
Michael Johnson	555-666-1212	michael.johnson@rivercity.gov	Access Granted	05-23-2017	Update Deny

If the user you are looking for isn't listed on the Authorize/Revoke Access screen, you would need to perform a search, like you did earlier. Michael's name is here, so we can select the **Update** link in the Action column to modify his access level.

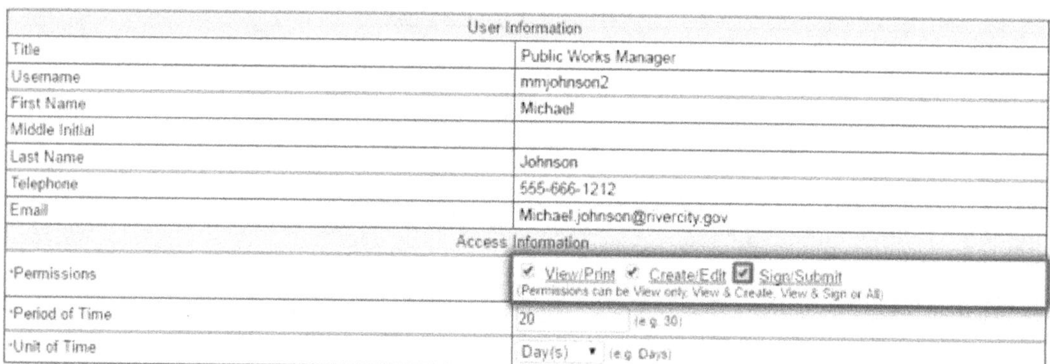

User Information		
Title	Public Works Manager	
Username	mmjohnson2	
First Name	Michael	
Middle Initial		
Last Name	Johnson	
Telephone	555-666-1212	
Email	Michael.johnson@rivercity.gov	
Access Information		
*Permissions	✔ View/Print ✔ Create/Edit ☑ Sign/Submit (Permissions can be View only, View & Create, View & Sign or All)	
*Period of Time	20 (e.g. 30)	
*Unit of Time	Day(s) ▼ (e.g. Days)	

We want to update his access to the Sign/Submit level, so let's select the **Sign/Submit** checkbox, in addition to the checkboxes for the lower levels.

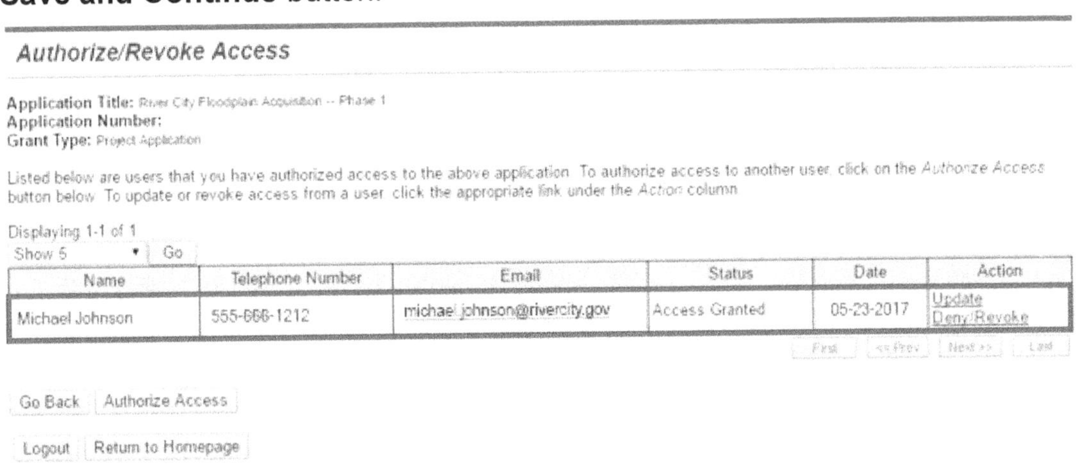

Just like when we provided Michael Create/Edit access to the application, you are going to need to enter a **justification** for updating his access. Type the explanation, "Promotion requires sign/submit responsibilities." Then select the **Save and Continue** button.

Michael Johnson now has Sign/Submit access and he can submit the floodplain acquisition subapplication to the State of Columbia on behalf of River City.

Revoking Access

From time to time, there may be a reason that you might need to revoke someone's access to a subapplication.

For example, if, instead of being promoted, Michael took a position in another city. He would no longer be working on the River City floodplain acquisition project, and he would not need access to the subapplication. Sally would need to revoke his access to the River City Floodplain Acquisition—Phase 1 subapplication in eGrants.

Sally will show you how to revoke an eGrants user's access.

Scroll down to see slideshow captions.

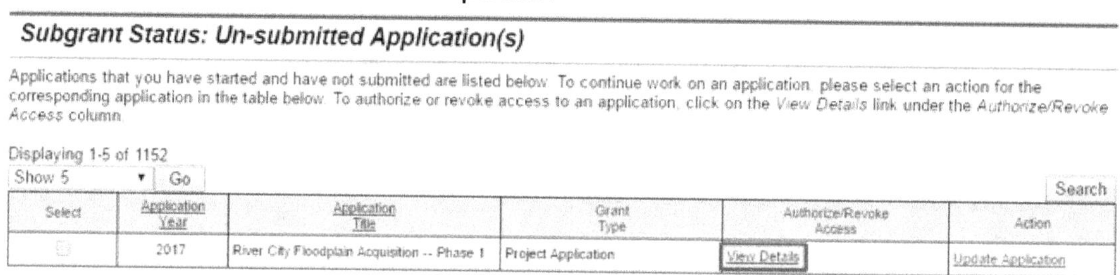

If Michael no longer worked for the River City government, then we would need to revoke his eGrants access to the floodplain acquisition subapplication. To revoke his access, start on the Subgrant Status: Un-submitted Application(s) screen. Find the River City Floodplain Acquisition—Phase 1 application title. Select the **View Details** link in the Authorize/Revoke Access column.

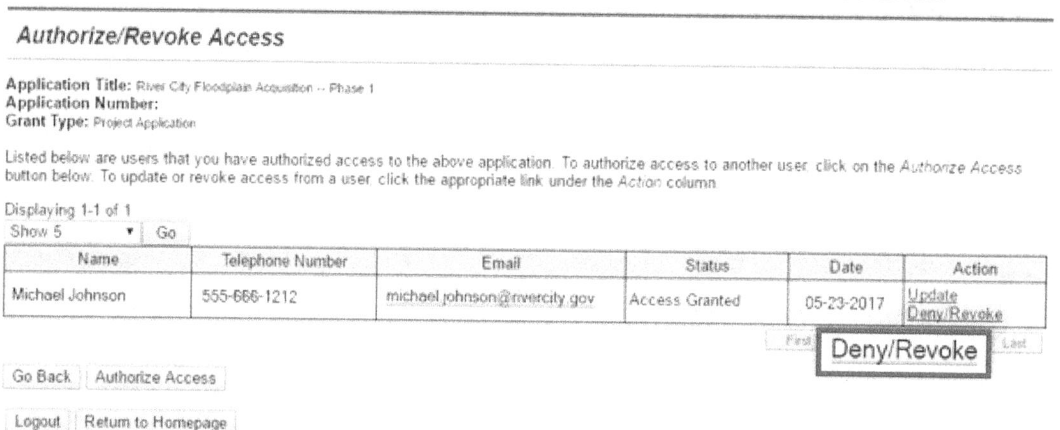

That takes us to the Authorize/Revoke Access screen. You now need to find Michael Johnson's name. You can see two links under the Action column on the far right: Update and Deny/Revoke. Select the **Deny/Revoke** link.

Application Title: River City Floodplain Acquisition -- Phase 1
Application Number:
Grant Type: Project Application

You have chosen to deny/revoke access from the following user for the above application.

User Information	
Title	Public Works Manager
Username	mmjohnson2
First Name	Michael
Middle Initial	
Last Name	Johnson
Telephone	555-666-1212
Email	Michael.johnson@rivercity.gov
Access Information	
·Permissions authorized	Create/Edit Sign/Submit View/Print
·Duration	20 DAYS
Comments	verification and advice

Are you sure you want to continue with this action?

No   Yes

A statement appears at the top of the screen confirming our revocation request and asking us to check the subapplication title and user name. To confirm our decision to revoke Michael's access to the River City Floodplain Acquisition—Phase 1 subapplication, select the **Yes** button. When his access is revoked, Michael's information will no longer appear on the Deny/Revoke Access screen.

Lesson 7 Summary

You have completed the lesson on how to manage access to subapplications you create.
In this lesson, you learned:

- eGrants users may provide individuals with access to subapplications, modify that access, or revoke the access.
- From lowest to highest, the access levels are: View/Print, Create/Edit, and Sign/Submit.
- An eGrants user may provide access to subapplications he or she has created to another user as long as the individual to whom the access is granted is within the same organization.
- The additional user's existing eGrants access level is the highest level of access he or she may be granted to any subapplication.
- A justification for granting, updating, or revoking an eGrants user's access must be provided.
- The time limit on an individual's access to a subapplication must also be indicated.

Lesson 8 Overview

At the end of this lesson, you will be able to:

- Identify the steps to update and submit a subapplication

Acquisition Scenario

Name: Sally Watkins
Community: River City, State of Columbia

Problem: Repetitive flooding of properties along the South Branch of the Washburn River

Proposed Solution: To acquire and demolish three properties

To Date: You have completed most of the River City Floodplain Acquisition—Phase 1 subapplication and have had Michael Johnson review it to confirm that information was entered correctly.

Listen to Sally
Audio transcript

Your Next Step: You must finish the final section of the subapplication section so that Michael can submit the subapplication on behalf of River City.

Hello. This is Sally and I wanted to let you know how much I appreciate your work on the subapplication. It is an important task because the subapplication is asking for funds to acquire and demolish three properties along the Washburn River that have repeatedly been flooded. I see you have filled out 13 sections of the subapplication. Now, I'm going to show you how to work on the remaining two sections. To do this, we first need to find the subapplication.

Un-Submitted Subapplications

When working on subapplications, many times you will not have all the information you need to complete a subapplication when you first create it. You will find that subapplications may be in different stages of development; some sections may be complete, while others may need more information.

eGrants allows you to create a subapplication, enter some information, save the subapplication, and then return to it at a later time to update and complete it.

Note It's always best to copy information from old, un-submitted subapplications to a new subapplication instead of updating the old, un-submitted subapplication. Copying information to a new subapplication ensures that the latest version of the subapplication is used and that it captures any changes made in eGrants to reflect current grant program guidance.

Searching for Un-Submitted Subapplications

eGrants allows you to search for existing subapplications to update. These are found under the **Update/Complete Un-Submitted Application** task menu option on the Subgrant Applicant Homepage because they have not yet been submitted to the Applicant. You and Sally have already created the River City Floodplain Acquisition—Phase 1 subapplication, and now you want to go back and enter additional data into it.

Sally is going to show you how to search for an un-submitted subapplication. Scroll down to see slideshow captions.

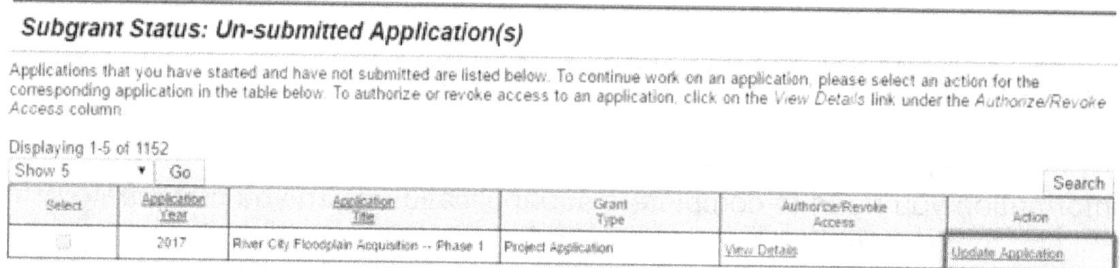

To locate an unsubmitted application, select the **Update/Complete Un-submitted Application** link on the Subgrant Applicant Homepage.

Subgrant Status: Un-submitted Application(s)

Applications that you have started and have not submitted are listed below. To continue work on an application, please select an action for the corresponding application in the table below. To authorize or revoke access to an application, click on the *View Details* link under the *Authorize/Revoke Access* column.

Displaying 1-5 of 1152

Show 5 ▼ Go | Search

Select	Application Year	Application Title	Grant Type	Authorize/Revoke Access	Action
☐	2017	River City Floodplain Acquisition -- Phase 1	Project Application	View Details	Update Application

Next, look for the name of the subapplication on the Subgrant Status: Un-submitted Application(s) screen. Since we are working on the River City

Floodplain Acquisition—Phase 1 subapplication, we want to select the **Update Application** link in the Action column for that subapplication title.

Application Section	Status
Subapplicant	Complete
Contact	Complete
Community	Complete
Mitigation Plan	Complete
Scope of Work	Complete
Properties	Complete
Schedule	Complete
Cost Estimate	Complete
Cost Share	Complete
Cost Effectiveness	Complete
Environmental/Historic Preservation	Complete
Evaluation	Complete
Assurances and Certifications	Complete
Comments and Attachments	Incomplete
Comments for FEMA	Incomplete

The Application Status screen appears. It lists all the sections of the subapplication and whether they are complete or incomplete.

Updating an Un-Submitted Subapplication

The Application Status screen lists the various sections in the subapplication. Next to each section, the status of that section is displayed as either "Incomplete" or "Complete." Before a subapplication is submitted, all sections must be complete (i.e., have a status of "Complete"). To update a section, select the **status link** to the right of the section name.

While working on a section of a subapplication, it is important to save your data by selecting either the Save or Save and Continue button at the bottom of the screen.

This screen shows the Status of the different sections of the full application. If the Status is Incomplete, you may click on the link to complete that section or you may use the menu on the left.

Application Section	Status
Subapplicant	Complete
Contact	Complete
Community	Complete
Mitigation Plan	Complete
Scope of Work	Complete
Properties	Complete
Schedule	Complete
Cost Estimate	Complete
Cost Share	Complete
Cost Effectiveness	Complete
Environmental/Historic Preservation	Complete
Evaluation	Complete
Assurances and Certifications	Complete
Comments and Attachments	Incomplete
Comments for FEMA	Incomplete

Go Back   Save and Continue

Select this link for the full text of the image.

Completing a Section

After completing each section of a subapplication, you will face a decision:

- If the subapplication is ready for submission, you may select **Review and Submit Application** link from the sidebar menu. Remember: Only users with Sign/Submit access in eGrants may submit a subapplication.
- If the subapplication is not ready for submission, you may select **Return to Home Page** link from the sidebar menu.

Select this link for the full text of the image.

Submitting a Subapplication

When all sections of a subapplication have a status of "Complete," the subapplication may be submitted to the Applicant. Only users with Sign/Submit access may submit a subapplication. The **Review and Submit** link in the sidebar menu facilitates this process.

Note   Always print the subapplication with the submission date and time for future reference.

Submitting a Subapplication (continued)

Sally has confirmed that the River City Floodplain Acquisition—Phase 1 subapplication is now ready for submission. Since Sally's co-worker, Michael Johnson, has Sign/Submit privileges for the subapplication, she has asked him to submit the subapplication on behalf of River City. Michael will show you the process.

Scroll down to see slideshow captions.

Print Blank Applications

Create New Application

Update/Complete Un-submitted Application(s)

Update/Complete Un-submitted Application

First, I need to locate the application in eGrants. On the Subgrant Applicant Homepage, I select the **Update/Complete Un-submitted Application** link.

Subgrant Status: Un-submitted Application(s)

Applications that you have started and have not submitted are listed below. To continue work on an application, please select an action for the corresponding application in the table below. To authorize or revoke access to an application, click on the *View Details* link under the *Authorize/Revoke Access* column.

Displaying 1-5 of 1152

Show 5   Go   Search

Select	Application Year	Application Title	Grant Type	Authorize/Revoke Access	Action
☐	2017	River City Floodplain Acquisition -- Phase 1	Project Application	View Details	Update Application

Then, I look for the River City Floodplain Acquisition—Phase 1 title on the Subgrant Status: Un-submitted Application(s) screen. I select the **Update Application** link in the Action column.

Application Status

Application 100% complete

This screen shows the Status of the different sections of the full application. If the Status is Incomplete, you may click on the link to complete that section or you may use the menu on the left.

Application Section	Status
Subapplicant	Complete
Contact	Complete
Community	Complete
Mitigation Plan	Complete
Scope of Work	Complete
Properties	Complete
Schedule	Complete
Estimate	Complete
Share	Complete
Cost Effectiveness	Complete
Environmental/Historic Preservation	Complete
Evaluation	Complete
Assurances and Certifications	Complete
Comments and Attachments	Complete
Comments for FEMA	Complete

Go Back   Save and Continue

I know that all the sections of the subapplication are complete and accurate. So, I can select the **Review and Submit Application** link from the sidebar menu on the left side of the screen.

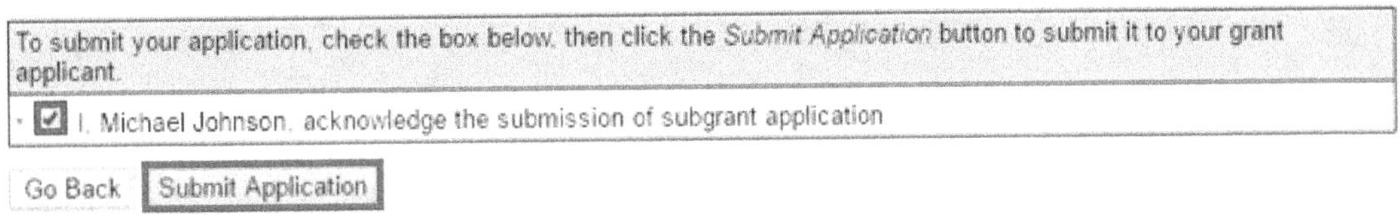

Then, I scroll down to the acknowledgement box at the bottom of the Review and Submit screen. There, I need to select the **checkbox** to indicate that I am signing the application. Finally, I select the **Submit Application** button.

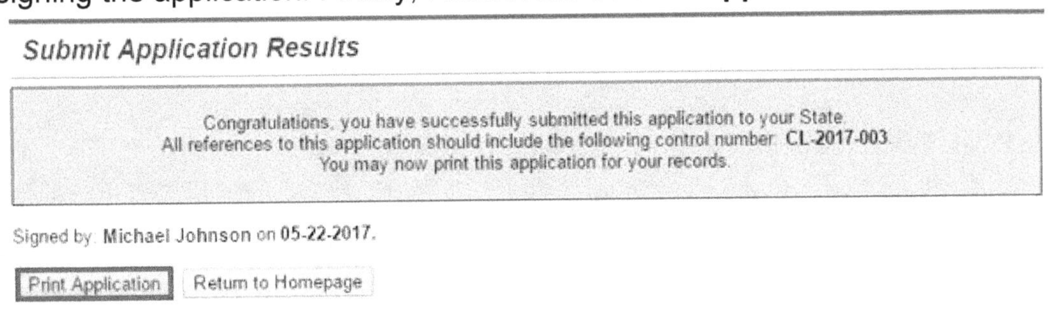

The Submit Applications Results screen displays the confirmation that the River City Floodplain Acquisition—Phase 1 subapplication was successfully submitted to the State of Columbia and provides the assigned control number for the subapplication. To keep a record of the submission, I need to select the **Print Application** button. It is important to keep a paper copy of the subapplication on file, along with the control number assigned to it.

Lesson 8 Summary

In this lesson you learned:

- You may begin a subapplication in one eGrants session and complete it in a different session
- When returning to eGrants to update a subapplication already begun, you should choose the Update/Complete Un-submitted Application link on the Subgrant Application Homepage
- To determine if a subapplication is complete, you should check the status of each section
- eGrants users must have Sign/Submit access to be able to submit a completed subapplication to an Applicant

Lesson 9 Overview

Upon completion of this lesson, you will be able to:

- Identify the steps to revise and resubmit a subapplication

Acquisition Scenario

Name: Sally Watkins

Problem: Sally works as City Manager in River City. Her current task is to assist the Mayor in finding funding for a large project. The project involves the purchase and demolition of three properties along the Washburn River. In past years, these properties have been repeatedly flooded. The Mayor wishes to ensure that these properties will not be flooded again and wants to reduce the impacts to families living in his community by seeking financial assistance to acquire the properties.

To date: You and Sally have worked together to complete and submit a subapplication for a subaward to help fund the project.

Listen to Sally
Audio transcript

Your Next Step: Sally has asked you to check the status of the subapplication.

Hello. It's Sally Watkins. Last month, we submitted a subapplication on behalf of River City to our Applicant, the Columbia Department of Emergency Management. Now, I'd like you to go back into eGrants to check the status of that subapplication. I will show you how to do it.

Subapplication Review Status

After a subapplication is submitted to the Applicant, it is a good idea to monitor the status of the subapplication as it is being reviewed by the Applicant—and then by FEMA, if the Applicant choses to submit it as part of its application. Some of the possible review status levels include:

Pending at Grantee—The subapplication has been submitted, but has not yet been reviewed by the Applicant for possible inclusion in its application.

Submitted to Stockpile—The subapplication was not selected to be included in the Applicant's application, but was retained by the Applicant for future consideration.

Approved by Grantee—The Applicant has approved the subapplication for inclusion in its application.

Attached to Grantee—The Applicant has included the subapplication in its application.

Revision Requested by Grantee—The subapplication is pending revision by the Subapplicant to address the Applicant's revision requests.

Submitted to FEMA—The Applicant submitted the subapplication as part of its application to FEMA.

Revision Released to Subgrantee—FEMA has reviewed a section or sections of a subapplication and has requested revisions to it, and the Applicant has released it for revision by the Subapplicant.

Approved by FEMA—FEMA has approved the subapplication and obligated it in a federal award to the Applicant.

Viewing the Status of a Subapplication

Sally will show you how to monitor the status of a submitted subapplication. Scroll down to view slideshow captions.

We should check on the status of the River City Floodplain Acquisition—Phase 1 subapplication after it has been submitted to the Applicant. Since the subapplication has been submitted, we need to select the **Revise/Amend Submitted Application(s)** menu option on the Subgrant Applicant Homepage.

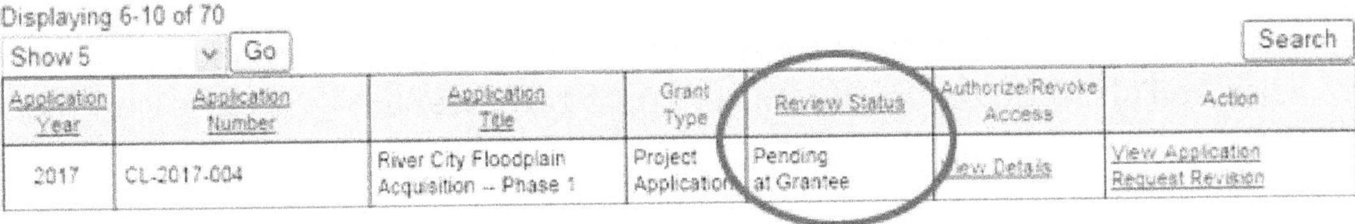

The Subgrant Status: Submitted Applications screen appears. The **Review Status** column displays the status of submitted subapplications. We can see that the status of the River City Floodplain Acquisition subapplication is **Pending at Grantee**, so the Applicant has not yet made a decision about it. We will need to check eGrants again in the near future to see if the subapplication status has changed.

Revision Requests

In some situations, you may need to make changes to a subapplication after you submitted it. For example, you would want to revise a subapplication if data changes, if a lower-cost solution is found, or if new information becomes available. Also, the Applicant may request a revision to the subapplication.

Once a subapplication is submitted, the information is "locked;" that is, no changes may be made to the subapplication without a revision request.

There are several types of revisions of a submitted subapplication that can be requested:

- An **Applicant** may request that a Subapplicant make revisions to a submitted subapplication.
- A **Subapplicant** may request that an Applicant return a submitted subapplication for revision. A Subapplicant should contact their Applicant official to request a revision.
- **FEMA** can also request that revisions be made to one or more sections of a subapplication that was submitted as part of an application. An Applicant could make revisions to the section(s) of the subapplication or could release the section(s) of a subapplication to the Subapplicant to make revisions.

Making Revisions Requested by an Applicant

If an Applicant wishes to request a revision to a subapplication, it must release a subapplication(s) to the Subapplicant so the revision can be made. On the Subgrant Status: Submitted Applications screen, this request for revision will show up as "Revision Requested By Grantee" in the Review Status column.

Once a subapplication section(s) has been released for revision, you would need to select **Update Application** in the Action column.

After selecting **Update Application,** you will see specific comments from the Applicant and have the opportunity to navigate to the subapplication section(s) to make the changes.

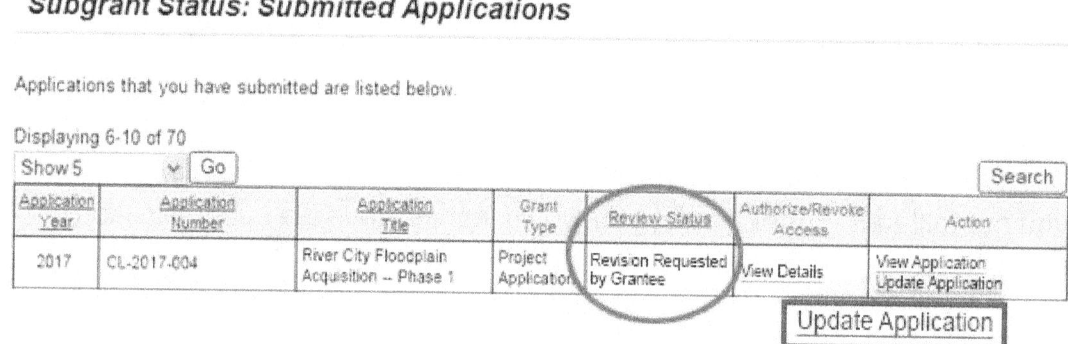

Select this link for the full text of the image.

Making Revisions Requested by FEMA

If a subapplication is included as part of an application to FEMA, there is the possibility that FEMA might request a revision to the subapplication. While some of these revisions can be made by the Applicant, other revisions must be completed by a Subapplicant. If a Subapplicant needs to make FEMA-requested revisions, the Applicant would have to create a revision request and release the section(s) of the subapplication to the Subapplicant. On the Subgrant Status: Submitted Applications screen, a revision request from FEMA will show up as "Revision Released to Subgrantee" in the Review Status column.

Once a subapplication section has been released, you would need to select Review Revision Request link in the Action column. You would then see specific comments about the requested revision(s). A section or sections of the subapplication will be unlocked so you would be able to make the changes.

Applications that you have submitted are listed below

Displaying 6-10 of 70

Show 5   Go   Search

Application Year	Application Number	Application Title	Grant Type	Review Status	Authorize/Revoke Access	Action
2017	CL-2017-004	River City Floodplain Acquisition -- Phase 1	Project Application	Revision Released to Subgrantee	View Details	View Application Review Revision Request

Review Revision Request

<u>Select this link for the full text of the image.</u>

Resubmitting a Subapplication

After the revisions are made and all sections of the subapplication show a "Complete" status, the subapplication may be resubmitted to the Applicant. The Review and Submit option in the sidebar menu facilitates this process. Remember: Only users with Sign/Submit access can resubmit a subapplication.

Sally has confirmed that the revisions made in each section are saved and the River City Floodplain Acquisition—Phase 1 subapplication is ready to be resubmitted by Michael.

☐	Properties	Complete
☐	Comments and Attachments	Complete
☐	Assurances and Certifications	Complete
☐	Forms	Complete
☐	Entire Application	Complete

To sign your application, check to box below and enter your password in the space provided. Then click the resubmit application button to resubmit your application to FEMA.

☑ I, Michael Johnson, acknowledge the submission of subgrant application.

Go Back   Resubmit Application

<u>Select this link for the full text of the image.</u>

Note   Always print the subapplication with the submission date and time for future reference.

Acquisition Scenario

Name: Sally Watkins

Problem: You have worked hard with Sally to create a subapplication for the proposed River City Floodplain Acquisition—Phase 1 project. The subapplication was submitted to the Applicant, the Columbia Department of Emergency Management, who later submitted a request to revise it. After revising and resubmitting it, Sally has now learned that the River City subapplication was included in the overall FMA application by the State of Columbia.

To date: The State of Columbia application, including the River City floodplain acquisition project subapplication, was approved by FEMA. Sally will now work with the State of Columbia officials to make sure she understands all of the subaward requirements before beginning the work.

<u>Listen to Sally</u>
<u>Audio transcript</u>

Hi. It's Sally Watkins. I have some good news! Our subapplication was included in the overall State of Columbia application to FEMA and was approved! Soon, River City is going to receive the funds to purchase and demolish the properties that are repeatedly flooded. Making a park in that area will minimize the impact of future flooding in our community. I'm so happy that everything worked out so well. Thank you for all your hard work in helping to prepare the subapplication!

Lesson 9 Summary

Congratulations! You have finished the final lesson in the Mitigation eGrants System for the Subapplicant Independent Study course! Some key points you learned in this lesson are:

- After submitting a subapplication, you should check on its review status.
- A Subapplicant may request an opportunity to revise an already-submitted subapplication.
- An Applicant may release a submitted subapplication for revision before it is included in an application.
- In response to a revision request by FEMA, an Applicant may release a section(s) of a subapplication to a Subapplicant for revision.
- Only users with Sign/Submit access may submit or resubmit a subapplication in eGrants.